Y

My
Preacher

Ron Karriker

Yours in Christ,

Ron Karriker

**A White Pastor's Gleanings
from a Cross-Racial Ministry**

10/13

Published by Sandime
8313 Long Island Road, Catawba, NC 28609

FIRST EDITION in ENGLISH

ISBN: 978-0-9717171-1-4

Library of Congress Control Number 2013913156

To protect the privacy of those people who have been a part of the author's life, some names have been changed.

Cover Art: Brian Policke

. . . Caucasians have also experienced racism as well as being racist, and persons of other ethnicities have been racist as well as having experienced racism.[1]

---

1   Quotation from an anonymous White clergywoman in McSpadden, Lucia. *Meeting God at the Boundaries*: *Cross-Cultural—Cross Racial Clergy Appointments*, Nashville, TN: General Board of Higher Education and Ministry of the United Methodist Church, 2003. (p. 59)

To My Friends

@

Scotts Chapel United Methodist Church
Philadelphia United Methodist Church

About the Author

Ron Karriker graduated from Lenoir-Rhyne College in 1964 with a degree in Religious Education. He holds an MHDL degree in Counseling from the University of North Carolina at Charlotte and a Master of Divinity degree from Hood Theological Seminary. He has held positions in social work, business management, and mental health counseling. In July 2013, he retired after 16 years as a Methodist minister.

Contents

FOREWORD

Seldom have I read a book that holds my attention to such an extent that I could hardly put it down until I read the last word. *You Ain't My Preacher* is that type of book.

Its author, Rev. Ron Karriker, makes it abundantly clear that this work is not the result of some copious, scholarly research but is a description of his reminiscences and reflections as a White American who had the courage to pursue his theological education in an historically Black seminary, and subsequently served for seven years as pastor of two African American, United Methodist congregations in the Piedmont area of North Carolina.

During those seven years of his pastoral appointment in that two-point charge, he had occasions when he was invited to consider transfers to pastor White and more financially secure congregations. On each occasion, having learned that there was uncertainty about who would succeed him, he offered to stay in the charge pastoring the people of those congregations that he had come to love and who had come to love him. He was deeply committed to the ministry of the church to which he felt called at a much earlier age but to which he committed his life in his fifties.

In an engaging and at times humorous manner, the author relates his many experiences of the most insidious, social problem we face in this country—racism—and shows that the problem is prevalent among many Whites and Blacks toward each other. He explains his preferred definition of that term as "hatred and intolerance of another race or races" (page 163). That explanation challenges the readers' self-examination regarding their attitude toward others who are different from them.

Ron's writing style is conversational to the extent that at times he writes in incomplete sentences rather typical of his preaching style. This easy style of writing engages the readers and enables them to enter into the experiences the author recounts. The most moving aspect of the book is to note the transformation that took place over time in the lives of the congregants he served, the pastors with whom he associated, and in him.

While not a textbook, it is a book that every person serving in a cross-racial appointment, or who intends to serve in such an appointment, or ministerial students in general ought to read, as the racial boundaries that once separated congregations are fast becoming an anachronism of the past. The communities the church serves today are much less racially defined, as they were a decade or two earlier. Hence, the affirmation of St. Paul—that **in Christ Jesus** "there is neither male nor female, bond or free, Jew or Gentile" (and we may add White or Black)— may be coming a reality in the church today.

It takes courage and honesty to write a book like this. In *You Ain't My Preacher,* Ron Karriker is continuing his ministry of reconciliation between White and Black Christians, and for this I highly commend him.

Albert J. D. Aymer
President
Hood Theological Seminary

Reflections in the Men's Room

August 30, 1994

Gazing at the single, curly, black hair in the men's room sink, I wondered: _What's an old White guy like me doing in this place?_

Lifting my head I stared at the mirror. Looking back at me was a man with nurtured racism as an adjunct of his southern-born, southern-raised childhood. A man who grew up in a time when use of the "N-word"[2] as a racial slur, even among children, was as common as ham and eggs and grits on the breakfast room table.

In the 1940s White kids often chanted a corrupt version of the classic ditty:

---

2   See Appendix, "The Terminology Dilemma," for a researched-based explanation of my usage of racial labels in this book.

Eeny, meeny, miny, moe.
Catch a [N-word] by his toe.
If he hollers let him go.
Eeny, meeny, miny, moe.

Every year at Christmastime my church gave out brown-paper, lunch bags filled with goodies: an orange, an apple, a banana (usually rotten), a candy bar, bubble gum, a small box of raisins, and an assortment of nuts: walnuts, pecans, and Brazil nuts which everybody called [N-word] toes.

Even as a child I knew that was wrong.

But when the Ku Klux Klan marched in the local Christmas parade, it had no meaning to me at all. There they were, every year, hoods and all, right behind the float with hounds baying and lunging at live 'possums clinging to a tree. A White Santa always ended the parade, throwing out pieces of candy to all the children, Black and White.

I couldn't understand why my daddy and uncles were always making derogatory remarks about anyone with dark skin. Or why my grandmother expressed fear that one of *those people* might break into her house and hurt her. But mostly I didn't think about race relations at all. Very early on I had the idea that if nobody's hurt me, why should I be concerned?

During my childhood no people of color lived within the limits of the small town where I went to school, and none were allowed to swim in the town's swimming pool. Relegated to working as maids, janitors, cooks, and field hands, they weren't even allowed to work in the town's cotton mills.

Customs and conventions established by White leaders demanded that Colored people sit at the back of public buses connecting small communities and sit in segregated balconies in movie theaters. Signs over public restrooms read, "Men" and "Women" and "Colored." Signs in restaurant windows read, "White Only." News accounts were segregated in the local paper where there was a special section titled, "Negro News and Activities."

The only place I knew of where teens of both races were allowed to congregate together was at the rock and roll shows held in the Charlotte Coliseum. Even then there was overt segregation. Negroes were required to sit on one side of the arena and Whites on the other.

Growing up in a rural area in the Piedmont section of North Carolina, I encountered only a few people of color during my childhood and teenage years. They included J. C., the school janitor; Otis, a neighborhood blacksmith; and a school bus driver whose name I never knew.

J. C. was every child's friend. He controlled the huge bell sitting at ground level that announced the start of school each day. If you asked, pleaded, or stayed close by, you might get the chance to pull the rope and receive a warm smile and a "thank you" from this man.

One day in our first-grade class, we heard a loud explosion coming from the nearby high-school building under construction. It was quite a shock when we learned that J. C. had been in that building when the boiler exploded.

It didn't matter what color the man was, he had been our friend.

Otis was my friend, too. I remember my daddy and his brothers saying things about the blacksmith like,

"That [N-word] can make anything out of metal."

"He's so talented. Pity he drinks so much."

"I hear he beats his wives."

Wives? Even as a kid I knew that a man was supposed to have only one wife.

When I was about seven or eight years old, my favorite uncle often took me to a little country store up the road a mile or two from my home. One day Otis was there. He smiled at me and then softly said something to my uncle. I couldn't hear what Otis said, but he went over to the drink box, picked up a 10-cent Coca Cola in a green glass bottle, and grabbed a hand-sized pack of shelled peanuts from a shelf. He paid the clerk then handed the Coke and peanuts to me.

I was hesitant to accept his gifts, not because of who he was, but because of what I had been taught: "Know who it is who offers you something."

Good advice, even for today.

My uncle smiled at me, so I took the treats from Otis and said, "Thank you, sir."

Otis smiled back.

I never knew what happened to Otis. One day he was there and then . . .

I never saw him again.

He was kind to me.

That's what I remember most.

My only Colored high school friend was a silent one. Like me, he drove a school bus. Schools in the South were still segregated in the 1950s. Buses from his school, Aggrey Memorial High School, ran some of the same routes as mine.

When our paths crossed we always waved and smiled at each other. Once when we met on a narrow road, one of us (I don't remember who started it) flipped out the metal stop sign attached just outside the driver's window.

The next day we both extended our signs as our way of greeting each other, resulting in a loud slam when they met. We laughed and waved at each other.

For a long time we did this daily.

How odd.

Two young men, both gregarious in nature, communicating by a silly action without words. How
might we have acted if we had met face to face? How
terribly sad that we were denied the opportunity to
know each other.

No Negroes were enrolled at Lenoir-Rhyne, the
small Lutheran college I attended in the early '60s.

During our sophomore year, I married Wanda,
my first-grade sweetheart. While still in school we
worked as houseparents at Sipe's Orchard Home, an
orphanage for boys. Few, if any, of the residents were
orphans. I never learned specific reasons why they
had been placed there, but I suspected it was because
of neglect and/or abuse or trouble with the law. All
were White.

I graduated in 1964 with a degree in Religious
Education—a perfect major to educate me for my 16
years in business management.

Wanda and I moved to Statesville, North Carolina. She taught school, and I worked at the Welfare
Department (now called the Department of Social Services). As a caseworker in the time when civil rights
marches and uproars were splitting the country, my
territory was in one of the poorest sections of town.

I had been told not to go there after dark, which
seemed logical to me. I had no intention of working at
night. Not for what I was getting paid.

When our children were born in 1965 and 1967, my salary was not enough to support a family, and I found a job as a management trainee in a large company.

As our children grew it was nice to be able to expose them to the activities that I enjoyed as a child. Weekend visits to my parents allowed them opportunities to ride on the tractor with me or in a wagon pulled by the tractor. They had fun helping their grandparents plant the garden, watching it grow, and eventually harvesting the produce. Walks in the woods and fishing and swimming in the pond were special to us all. But an ugly thing threatened to ruin those visits—

Bigotry!

One day my dad used the [N-word] in the presence of the young impressive ears of my children.

"Dad. Please don't talk that way in front of your grandchildren."

"If they're gonna be spendin' time with me, they're gonna hear it," he screamed.

You would've thought I'd asked him to give up his freedom of speech entirely.

I replied with reason: "My children will grow up in a different world from what you did. It's changing fast. I don't want them to be prejudiced by the things we say or do."

Even louder he repeated what he'd just said as if I hadn't heard him. "If they're gonna be spendin' time with me, they're gonna hear it."

"Well Dad, I can remedy that," I said with palpable anger in my voice.

He got the point and my ultimatum was never mentioned again.

Neither did he ever again utter the [N-word] around my family or me.

In 1970 we moved from Statesville and I began my climb up the corporate ladder in a company sensitive to racial issues and supportive of affirmative action for hiring minorities.

In the early '80s I left this job, briefly worked as a management consultant, then entered a graduate program in counseling, obtaining an MHDL (Master of Human Development and Learning) degree. During this experience at the University of North Carolina at Charlotte, I encountered no Black students or professors.

For several years I worked as a mental health counselor in Wanda's private psychological practice. In this capacity I also did contract work for a local school system, working with inner city, high-risk kids. Most were African American.

I enjoyed working as a helping professional but became restless. A stirring in my soul—again—driving me toward something I couldn't see.

Oh, I had an idea of what it was, but that was over.

Or so I thought!

Returning to the present I glanced back down at the single, curly, black hair in the men's room sink.

It must be true. God definitely has a sense of humor. What else could explain how I, a 54-year-old man, could find myself the only White student at Hood Theological Seminary?

The Journey

First Call – Adolescence

Lutheranism had been my family's religion all the way back to the Black Forest region of Germany. It was so ingrained in my life that I wondered if we should call Reformation Sunday, "To heck with Roman Catholics Day."

Hey! If Roman Catholics kicked Martin Luther out of their church, they couldn't be too smart. I spent three years in catechetical classes studying *Luther's Small Catechism*, waiting for my first communion, memorizing creeds, studying the Augsburg Confession, and being screamed at by our pastor who had no patience with preteens and teenagers.

Those were years of working in the fields, helping at the barn, hunting in the woods, and growing in my faith. I still wonder how that happens—growing in faith as a child. I guess it's easier than in later years.

As much as eating and breathing, religion was part of my life.

I never thought about *not* going to church on Sundays, I just went.

I never thought about *not* going to Luther League, I just went.

I never thought about *not* going to choir practice, I just went.

I liked church activities. So many different things to do: Easter cantatas and Christmas programs; hayrides and hot dog roasts with the youth group; holding hands in the graveyard with my first girlfriend. (Well, the graveyard was *on* the church grounds.)

Then one day he was there—the first person to profoundly influence my spiritual life. I was fifteen years old. Pastor Paul Conrad, fresh out of seminary, came to our 400+ member rural church. He was young, fun-loving, people-oriented, and musically inclined. The polio epidemic of the late 1940s had left him paralyzed from his waist down, and he walked on Canadian crutches and drove his car with hand controls.

At last we had a pastor who could communicate with anybody—one who understood who *I* was. He filled in a lot of gaps that my harsh father should have provided, and he made me feel that I was worthy of God's grace.

From Pastor Paul I learned that religion does not always have to be serious. Surely God must have loved the boogie-woogie music he banged out on the church piano after he had me check to make sure no one else was around. And he was a lot of fun at our youth group's meetings and parties.

In this atmosphere of freedom I grew in my faith.

One Sunday Pastor Paul did something different, something that I'd never seen happen in our church. I'd heard that the Baptists up the road did it. After his sermon he stood in our holy pulpit telling people they needed to be closer to God, to listen to His call.

"Come to the altar," he beckoned.

I followed his call and went to the front of the sanctuary and knelt by the piano. Listening to organ music coming from the other side of the church, I began crying.

What's the matter with me? Men don't cry like this— not in public, not in church for heaven's sake!

Then I did something I'd never done before. I turned loose. I gave up control and opened myself to whatever feeling should come upon me. On that day the Lord called me to His service as a minister of the Gospel. I knew I should preach the Word.

Later I told Pastor Paul about my decision to become a Lutheran minister. And since I'd not told my parents, I asked him not to tell anyone about it.

Did he listen?

No.

During his sermon the next week he announced to the entire congregation that Ron Karriker had felt the call to ministry.

Why?

The one person I trusted to talk with about my spiritual plight and growth gets all hyped-up in an emotional outburst and tells the whole congregation what I'd shared in confidence.

When families gathered with their respective clans for Sunday dinner, they had something fresh to chew on. That's the kind of news that would've kept the telephone party lines humming during the following week.

"Hey, did you hear? That Karriker boy's gonna be a preacher."

"I guess Bessie and Roy sure are proud, I reckon."

Bessie and Roy proud? I'm not sure that's completely true. How proud can you be to hear something like that about your offspring at the same time that three hundred others hear it?

In quiet times of introspection I reflect on that altar call at the Lutheran church. Even now I smile as I recall a conversation years later with Pastor Paul. "Why did you do it?" I had asked.

"I remember it well," he answered. "The feeling to have an altar call came upon me without thought, without reason, and I just did it. I gave the invitation, closed my eyes, and prayed. When I opened my eyes, it seemed as if every person in the sanctuary was standing as close to the altar as space would allow."

"How did you feel about that?" I asked.

With his characteristic sense of humor Pastor Paul answered: "I remember praying again, saying something like, 'Lord, you got them up here. Now what do I do with them?'"

No Call – Young Adulthood

I rebelled.

In my senior year of high school my dad had insisted I stay home and attend a small college within twenty-five miles of our home.

No way!

See, there was this girl. Wanda and I had been dating since our junior year in high school.

I loved her; I told her.

She laughed.

I think it scared her.

She was going to Lenoir-Rhyne College and I couldn't stand to be away from her, so I applied to the Lutheran school as a pre-theological student.

Dad wouldn't have it! I was supposed to stay home—to remain within his realm of control. He griped, "I can't afford to send you up there. If you go to that place, I won't give you one red cent."

I went anyway.

In my second year in college, I began having doubts about my spiritual calling. Is this what I really wanted to do?

Catch that?

Is this what *I* wanted to do? I'd completely left out one part of the equation. God undoubtedly had nothing to do with this. At least I never consulted God about it. It was how *I* felt.

Dr. Wade F. Hook, a Lutheran pastor and my sociology professor, empathized with me as I explained that I wasn't sure of my call any longer and that I needed help in sorting out answers to some questions. He reminded me of a scheduled meeting with the President of the North Carolina Synod of the Lutheran Church in America.

Each year the Lutheran leader, along with a whole room full of aged men in black shirts with clerical collars (or as Pastor Paul would have described them, "with their halos hanging around their necks") would descend upon the campus to talk with the Lutheran pre-theological students. If we qualified, the synod would grant money each year toward our tuition. If we stayed in the synod for four years after graduating from seminary, our debts would be forgiven.

I had looked forward to talking with the venerable exegetes of the Word when they came to inspect their investments. I wanted to seek their wisdom and ask for answers to questions about my future.

The day came and Dr. Hook ushered me into a small room. He pointed to my seat at a large oval table and introduced me to all present.

The synod president wasted no time in asking: "You've decided not to enter the ministry?"

Apparently Dr. Hook had already told the group about my concerns.

"Y-Yes sir," I stammered. "I'm having doubts. I have some questions I'd like to ask."

The president ignored my request and continued with his agenda.

"How much money have we given you?"

I was taken aback. Who cares how much money? I had things to discuss. How much money? I regained control, made eye contact with the man, and answered slowly, "None. Not one red cent."

"None?"

"Yes sir. None."

"Thank you, Mr. Karriker." The president looked at his secretary. "Who's next?"

I was shattered. I had gone to Mecca to receive enlightenment. I had climbed the mountain to the temple to learn the truth. I had gone to the church leaders seeking help.

I was worried about my future.

They were worried about money.

My mind went into overdrive.

Well, to heck with it all! If they don't care, why should I? I suppose I was wrong in the beginning. Guess God didn't really call me. I was caught up in a moment of emotionalism. That's all.

What should I do now? What career to follow?

Wanda was still with me. Seems she always had been. The one constant in my life, the one dependable object, the one person I could never live without, she was there. The world had suddenly become more closed and cruel.

What should we do now?

We got married!

She was nineteen; I was twenty.

We worked at various jobs to pay for our tuition, rent (except when we worked at the orphanage for food and housing) and even buy a car.

I obtained my degree without one red cent from my dad or the Lutheran synod.

At a family cookout after I had graduated, I heard my dad say to his brothers, "Now that we got that boy out of college, maybe I can get some things we need around here."

I bit my lip and walked away.

When we moved to Statesville to begin my work at the Welfare Department, we joined a small Lutheran church about the time their pastor was moving to another church. I was appointed to the pulpit committee.

Our job was to travel around listening to preachers to see if we could find a good one. I remembered Pastor Paul of my teenage years. He had left my home church after I left for college. I'd been in touch with him and knew he was ready to move again, so I suggested him to the committee. They liked his personality and preaching style and called him to preach at our church.

This time Pastor Paul came into my life more as a friend and mentor than an authority figure. Not knowing that I would ever need it, he modeled for me what a Christian minister should be.

Second Call – Middle Age

Don't ask me how I knew this.

When I was 52 years old, I came to believe I needed to search for my place in God's plan. All I can say is that it was one of those thinking, feeling, and knowing things.

But what did it mean?

How do you begin to look for something when you're not sure what you're looking for? I suppose it's one of those "I'll know what it is when I find it" episodes in our lives. Let's call it "my purpose in life."

The Lutheran church was not where I would find my reason to be in God's world. I had been a Lutheran all my life, and I knew I had to leave. No ill will or feelings toward Lutheranism or anyone in the denomination, but I was certain I had to embark on a different path.

One night I was startled awake with the scripture verses printed below running through my mind. I sat straight up in bed, kicked off the covers, and literally ran to my home office. I took a Bible from the bookshelf and read:

> [26]Consider your own call, brothers and sisters: not many of you were wise by human standards, not many were powerful, not many were of noble birth. [27]But God chose what is foolish in the world to shame the wise; God chose what is weak in the world to shame the strong; [28]God chose what is low and despised in the world, things that are not, to reduce to nothing things that are, [29]so that no one might boast in the presence of God. (I Corinthians 1: 26-29 from *New Revised Standard Version*)

Crying and laughing at the same time, I hurried back to our bedroom to awaken Wanda. She probably thought I had finally "lost it." I explained what had just happened and we spent the remainder of the night discussing what those words were telling me:

I'm good enough. No matter the things I've done wrong in the past, no matter not being able to satisfy everyone in my past, God can use me. God can use the foolish and the weak, the low and despised for God's purpose.

God can use me, too.

Yes, God, the decision is made.

I will follow where you lead.

Looking Over the Field

What to do now?

I set out to learn about different denominations.

On Sunday mornings and Sunday and Wednesday evenings, I attended services in various denominations: Baptist (both Black and White), Church of Christ, Church of God, Church of the Nazarene, Disciples of Christ, Episcopal, Anglican Church, Foursquare Gospel, Presbyterian (both Black and White), United Methodist Church (UMC), and a Pentecostal Holiness church.

I would listen, observe, and talk with the pastors, giving myself time and opportunity to learn more about the theology and practices in various churches. I was also giving God the time and opportunity to guide me as God wished. God didn't need me to do this, but it helped me to reason my way through it all.

Following are some examples of experiences at the beginning of my journey.

1. The "Lost List"

Before I stepped through that door, I didn't realize how lost I was.

The first church I visited on my journey to wherever I was headed was a small Independent Baptist Church. About 20 White adults were present at the

Sunday morning service. They appeared to be good, down-to-earth people. A majority of them had probably worked in the local cotton mills most of their lives. Good Christian folk. Salt-of-the-earth types. They made me feel welcome.

The music was standard fare for a conservative Baptist church. Before the sermon, delivered by an aging pastor, they discussed something called a "Lost List." I had no idea what kind of list they were talking about.

At the Wednesday evening service I learned the reason for the list. It was made up of names of church members, past members, friends, and acquaintances who, by their actions and lifestyles, had made it plain that they were indeed lost souls—souls bound for hell because they committed such terrible sins as mowing the lawn on Sunday, buying a six-pack of beer (a clear clue to the fact the purchaser actually drank this devil's brew), going to movies on Sunday evening when they should have been in church asking forgiveness for their sins, swearing, and (it seemed to me) having too much fun in life.

Dear God, I wondered. *Do I belong on that list? Over my life, I've committed most of those sins . . . and more.*

Tobacco was once my demon. Even used it as a child. Sucked its smoke into my lungs and chewed it when working outside, a common practice on the farm. My dad and uncles smoked. My grandfather chewed.

I began smoking on Boy Scout camping trips when I was 12 years old. In the days when it was not illegal for children to buy cigarettes, we'd buy them at the country store and smuggle them into the campground. If we ran out, our scoutmaster would give us one every now and then.

I was 14 years old when I learned how harmful cigarettes are to your body. I'd hidden a pack of Winstons in the dresser drawer in my room. Mother found them and told Dad. He dragged me to a shed in the backyard, grabbed a leather whip he used to train dogs, and proceeded to strike me with it.

Again and again.

I did my best to show no reaction.

"Stop it! Stop!" I heard my mother scream.

My dad did not comply.

I could only imagine my mother's feelings of horror and helplessness.

I continued to smoke throughout high school and college and for a couple decades afterwards. When I finally decided to quit, I was up to two packs a day.

Having used tobacco was much worse than mowing the lawn or going to the movies on Sunday.

I wasn't good enough for this congregation; therefore, I didn't return. I didn't want my name to be posted on anybody's "Lost List."

2. Like a Barroom Brawl

My visit to another Baptist church, a small frame house that had been converted to a place of worship, turned out to be quite entertaining.

Walking toward the church, I happened to glance and see about 20 feet away in the yard next door, a bikini-clad, bleached-blonde lying on her stomach reading a book. She had untied the bikini top. I guess she was trying to rid herself of those ugly stripes caused by those tiny little strings.

She looked toward me and smiled.

With the bathing beauty outside, I wondered what might be inside.

Something interesting perhaps?

Yes indeed.

When I walked through the door, about a dozen White men and women turned and stared at me. Unlike the cheery welcoming committee outside in the sun, no one smiled.

I sat on the back pew and waited for the service to begin. The musician announced a song. Apparently, the preacher didn't like her choice. They argued about what to sing and ended up screaming at each other.

I had been entertained enough, so I stood up and walked out. On the way to my truck, I glanced again at the young lady in the string bikini.

She gave me a knowing smile and went back to her book.

There are too many fights to be fought in life. One should not have to fight in church. I don't attend a worship service to quibble over which song to sing. I'm sure God enjoys them all when sung with an attitude of praise.

As a child, fighting in church meant more than having arguments. One of my pastors was a fighter, literally. He had married into the Karriker family. Fit right in, it seems.

As the story goes, during a church council meeting a heated argument ensued. Apparently the pastor didn't like something one of his wife's relatives had said, and this man of the cloth picked up a wooden chair and "went at him."

Now, according to some of the witnesses, the victim may have needed "a good stomping," but it would have looked a little better if the preacher had waited until after the council meeting.

Need to take care of God's work first, you know.

I didn't visit any other Baptist churches. Nothing against them. I grew up with Baptists and went to Vacation Bible School at the Baptist church in my community. To join a Baptist church, I would have had to be baptized again which meant being immersed. I have nothing against immersion. In fact, I believe it is the method that is most symbolic of what baptism represents. But I was baptized as a child using the sprinkle method and, in my opinion, one baptism is enough regardless of how much water is used.

3. Not Meant to Be

Knowing little about Presbyterianism except that it is based on the tenets of John Calvin, I decided to check out the Presbyterians. I had heard the word "predestination" and also the quizzical term "double-barrelled predestination" associated with this denomination.

On a weekday morning I stopped by the Second Presbyterian Church in a nearby town to see if I could talk with its pastor. Walking toward the pastor's office door, I played with the church's name.

Second Presbyterian Church. Second! The First Presbyterian Church must be bigger and better and closer to the middle of town. To me, Second Presbyterian Church sounds like a putdown. I wonder if there is a Third Presbyterian Church or Fourth? What kind of self-image would a person have being a member of the Second Presbyterian Church? Would it be possible for this congregation to work hard and climb the ecclesiastical ladder to become number one?

The pastor wasn't in and that was all right with me. I didn't want to talk with a preacher whose self-esteem might not be very high, being number two and all.

I later visited a Presbyterian church in a rural setting. The sanctuary was almost full of worshipers, and I had to search for a place to sit. The service was fine. The music was beautiful. The pastor was a good preacher.

After the service everyone left, and no one even said "Hello" to me—no one except the pastor. He knew I was a visitor. Later he sent a card. But not one other person in the entire church had even said "Hello."

I suppose I was not predestined to become a Presbyterian.

4. Sojourn in a Pentecostal Church

A neighbor whose life exemplifies the adage, "Her life is the best sermon I've ever seen," invited me to her Pentecostal Holiness church. I had never been to one before. Never even thought about Pentecostalism that much. Having been reared a Lutheran, that didn't seem like the kind of place I would be accepted or happy.

Wrong.

People in her church welcomed me warmly. No questions asked.

Some had come from Georgia years before. An elderly gentleman explained to me: "We followed the train hauling the cotton we raised to see where it went. The train stopped in Kannapolis, right across the street from Cannon Mills. And so did we. Been here ever since."

I joined their church. I loved the spiritualism, the openness, and the expectations they had that God was with them in church, and that good things were about to happen.

I occasionally heard people speaking in tongues. Not anything dramatic, it just happened. Fellow church members always reacted calmly to what some people in mainline churches might call an aberration. They listened, gave the voices time to be heard, and continued with the service.

Their pastor allowed me in their pulpit to preach. I will always be grateful for that.

They had expectations. Since I felt I was called to preach, they encouraged me to follow the call; let God have his way in my life.

I sometimes preached at the Wednesday evening service. I taught Sunday School for a while and sang in the choir. I witnessed many good things that still make me wonder what and how they happened.

Expectations!

When I told the pastor I planned to enter seminary, he said, "I don't understand why you need to go to seminary. God will lead you into God's way."

"I believe God is leading me to seminary," I said.

"Then go," he said.

Heeding the Call

Dr. Doris Weddington, a Methodist minister, succinctly described the next part of my journey when she preached the following sermon, reprinted here in a format similar to the one she used for her sermon notes.

Sermon
for
"Pastor Appreciation Sunday"
at
Philadelphia UMC
December 17, 2000
Ron Karriker, Pastor

(Part 1)

Genesis 12: 1 and 4

Abraham was living a settled life in Haran.
    Haran was his home.
        Everybody knew him and he knew everybody.
    He worshiped God as his forefathers had done.
        The ways of this city—this area—were familiar.
        He knew what was expected of him
            and what he could expect from others.
    It was a comfortable situation—a comfortable life.

Then came a stirring in his soul—a restlessness.
    He couldn't understand it, but something inside was saying:
        "Get up and move!"
    And God said, "Go from your country and your
        kindred and your father's house."
    And did God tell him where he was going?
        No!
    God said,
        "Leave here not knowing where you will settle again.
        Leave here not knowing what your future holds.
        Leave here on faith."

And then in verse 4, these words: "SO ABRAM WENT!"
    God said, "GO!" and Abram WENT!
        Abram was 75 years old.

In Hebrews we read:
    "By faith Abraham obeyed when he was called to set out for
    a place that he was to receive as an inheritance, and

HE SET OUT, NOT KNOWING WHERE HE WAS GOING."

And Hebrews goes on to say, "He lived in tents."
    Temporary lodging.

Moving from place to place.
Trusting God would somehow lead him to the place
   God wanted him to be.
   A place where he could settle in the center of God's will
     in the PROMISED LAND.

I know a man living today who took such a journey.

He had always attended a church of the denomination in which
his father and several generations of ancestors had worshiped.

Here, he was on familiar territory.
He knew the forms of worship, the ways—the customs.
He knew what was expected of him and what he could expect
   from others.
The church was his home—
   a comfortable situation,
   a comfortable place to live his church life.

Then one day there was a stirring in his soul.
   A restlessness began to grow.
He couldn't understand it, but something inside was saying:
   "GET UP AND MOVE! I need you somewhere else.
   There is a PROMISED LAND where I want you to go,
     and work I want you to do."

And did God tell this man where he was going?
   NO!
As it was with Abraham, God said,
   "Leave here not knowing where you will settle again
     or what service it is you must do."

God said, "GO!" and RON KARRIKER WENT!

Ron was then 52.

What happened after that is a long story.
    I can't possibly give you the full details today.

This man explored.
    There was a hunger in his heart . . .
        hunger for a place of worship where the presence of
            the Spirit was NOT just TALKED about,
            but EXPERIENCED,
        where the people were free to EXPRESS
            their joy in the Lord,
        where the Bible was studied seriously,
        where the fullness of God's word was preached, and
        where his soul would be
            satisfied,
            content,
            no longer restless—
                a place of service,
                a place of challenge.

And for a while Ron "lived in tents,"
    visiting for a while at one church and then another,
    searching for the
        PROMISED LAND.

Meanwhile this man began to hear whispers in his spirit:
    a still small voice.
Was he hearing things?

Sometimes he <u>thought</u> God's voice was saying:
    "I want you to <u>preach</u> my word and <u>shepherd</u> my people."

And Ron answered,
    "WHO? ME? But there are so many barriers that could
    never be overcome."

About this time, Ron did something he hadn't done in ten years or more. He took a notion he himself could not understand. He got up on a Sunday morning and went to the Karriker family reunion —

NOT one of his favorite ways to spend most of a Sunday.

Present at the reunion was a woman preacher in her sixties.

She had the devotional and asked the blessing before the meal.
        Then, although they were strangers to each other,
                she *just happened* to sit down across the table from him.

He felt moved to talk with her.
After the meal, he asked her for a few minutes of her time.
He shared with her about his journey — his yearning —
        his growing sense of calling and
        his questions and doubts.

The woman preacher assured him that what he was feeling
        rang true with her own experience of calling.
She, too, had received the call in her fifties.

God pays no attention to age.

Look at Abraham, called at 75 to leave home for God only knew where. And Moses, who heard God's call from the burning bush at the age of 80.

Like Ron, this woman preacher had already come through two careers. The gospel ministry was her third.

Remember . . . when Amos heard God's call?
        He was a herdsman and a dresser of sycamore trees.

Peter was a fisherman; Matthew, a tax collector.

Like Ron, she had left a familiar church after 47 years—and changed denominations to follow God's call.

The woman promised to pray for Ron as he continued on his journey.

There remained for this man—for Ron—the fact that there was no possible way he could attend seminary. There was no seminary near enough.

He was saying to God,
      "If this call is real, show me how I can go to seminary."

Then something else *just happened*.

Wanda needed a certain book and Ron offered to locate a copy.

He inquired at a university library. The librarian put out a computer search. The only copy of this book in the State of North Carolina was in a library only 25 miles from Ron's home:

HOOD THEOLOGICAL SEMINARY in Salisbury, NC.

A seminary in Salisbury? One he didn't even know existed.

What do you think?
      Did this *just happen*?
            OR
      Was it the HAND OF GOD?

Still exploring to find his church home, Ron enrolled at Hood — the only White student in an otherwise all-Black seminary.

There was a period of adjustment as the other students got used to Ron and Ron got used to them.

But since Ron has not an ounce of prejudice in his system and since his love for everybody is so real, the relationships soon became easy, and everybody forgot color altogether.

For three years Ron studied, thought, and prayed as he and fellow students shared their problems, hopes, and dreams together.

He attended worship in the chapel and found in the worship there many of the qualities his spirit longed for.

At some point during his second year of seminary, Ron
    sought out the woman preacher again,
    visited her congregation for a while,
    felt he could make this church his home,
    and made his commitment to the United Methodist Church.

By this time, his calling was strong and unmistakable.
    And he prayed.
He told the Lord he had no interest in becoming famous
    or preaching in big churches
    or getting big salaries.

What he prayed for was simply the opportunity to preach the Word and be a pastor to a family of God's people.

YOU . . . and the members at Scotts Chapel . . . are the answer to his prayer.

Wandering in A Strange Land

In this section I share some of my most memorable experiences as the only White student (and to my knowledge the oldest full-time student) during my three-year tenure at Hood Theological Seminary.

1. Crossing Racial Boundaries

R. K. Journal Entry: 08-30-94

Now I know how a beautiful woman feels when her fellow human beings stare at her. It's my first day at Hood, the beginning of seminary studies. I, too, have been stared at on this day and not because I'm beautiful, but because I'm an oddity in this place—the only Caucasian student.

My fellow students and the professors seemed surprised and guarded. One of my professors, Dr. Smith, was a real treat to meet. He and I are about the same age, but I feel young in intelligence next to him. His teaching style is different from what I've experienced in the past. In fact, this entire situation is different than anything I have ever experienced.

Dr. Smith is robust in his teaching. He's also a shouter with a somewhat aggressive style. He kept glancing at me throughout the class period as if worried he would offend me in some manner.

After class he called me aside to have a few private words. He appeared to be having a difficult time telling me he was sorry if he had insulted me earlier.

"I hope I didn't say something in class that might make you think I'm a racist," he said.

I had heard nothing of the sort, but he kept talking, using a lot of energy trying to convince me he was not a racist.

Doth he protest too much?

This man was never offensive to me. His apology for something he wasn't sure he had done foreshadowed some of the racially-loaded phenomena I would face after crossing the boundary from my White world to Hood's Black world.

2. We All Need a Friend to Lean On
R. K. Journal Entry: 09-01-94

Someone called me "Brother" today!

In those early days "in the Hood" (as some of the students affectionately called the seminary), the majority of my classmates were kind and helpful to me and tried to make me feel welcome. But in a strange environment with unfamiliar people quite different from me, I needed a special friend and found one in Brother T.

Maybe Brother T. was looking for a friend, too.

This young man was from a New England state and a member of the AME Zion Church which owned and operated Hood. He had heard the lion roar, had heard God call him to the ministry, and his bishop had suggested that he enroll at Hood. He, his lovely wife, and precocious, early school-aged child had transplanted to the South to a strange place.

They lived upstairs in the seminary's main building (a large building that housed classrooms, administrative offices, the library, and a few small apartments for students).

We first met one early morning. Brother T. was unlocking the main door for the building, a task he did each day as a student employee of the school. We had most of our classes together and often ate together. Sometimes he ate with his other friends and I ate alone.

Most mornings I enjoyed interacting with Brother T.'s daughter as she waited on the school bus. Once around Christmastime, I had tried to amuse her by doing my rendition of Santa Claus.

"Ho, Ho, Ho," I said in my deepest voice.

"You're not Santa. Santa's Black!" She was adamant in her response.

Although I had a good laugh at this, Brother T. scolded his daughter for being disrespectful to me.

"It's okay," I winked at the child. "I know your Santa is Black."

Her Santa is Black.

Mine is White.

Always had been.

Always would be.

Perhaps that's the main reason people of different races don't get along like we should. We see things from our own perspective. Therefore, Black is not always Black. It can also be White.

How will we ever get it right?

3. Me? A Token?

Two weeks after I had entered Hood as its only White student, I was elected vice-president of my class. Turned it down. The following notes from my journal remind me that I later changed my mind:

R. K. Journal Entry: 09-22-94

After the class president talked with me, I decided to accept the V. P. office. At lunch a new friend, who had been quite vocal to the class president about my serving, remarked how happy he was that I took the office.

"Why does it matter to you?" I asked.

"Because it's good for Hood," he answered. "Gives us the opportunity to show our diversity, to show that our seminary is an open place."

"Okay. I understand where you're coming from."

But what I really understood was that he wants me as V. P. because I'm White—he wants to "show me off."

I'm a token. Over 50 and White!

I felt used, wondering if they had a quota system to meet.

Although I was certain that my friend, Brother T., wasn't being nice to me because I was White, at times I wondered if there was an organized effort by other Hood students to make me feel at home—like when someone asked me to join the seminary choir. I declined. I'd heard them sing, and they didn't need me.

4. Invisible

In my first year, I quickly learned how it felt to be ignored and looked down upon. I would often eat lunch at the local Western Sizzlin. It was typical for other students to come into the restaurant, push a couple tables together, go through the buffet line, eat, laugh, and talk loudly. They usually sat within five or six feet of me and never acknowledged my existence.

Never a "hello."

Never an invitation to join the conversation.

Always exclusion.

Even when Brother T. was sitting at the table with the group of African Americans, and I entered the restaurant, they never invited me to join them.

Years later when I mentioned to Brother T. about my having been ignored at the Western Sizzlin, he was shocked. He had never noticed the shunning.

5. Will the Real Racist Please Stand Up?

Racism knows no color barrier. Although I was the target of racial slurs at Hood, especially in my first year by upperclass students who never got to know me, I also heard racist statements from my White friends and certain members of my family.

An elderly relative, speaking about my class-mates, was serious when she asked, "How can you tell them apart?"

When a clergy friend found out I was going to an all-Black school, he asked, "Why are you going to *that* school?"

A minister's wife asked me, "How are you doing academically in seminary?"

"Fine. Making better grades than I did in college."

"Well, going to *that* school I'd expect you to."

On my first day at Hood, I had met a woman who was also beginning seminary. Angela was married to a local politician and they had three young children. I sat behind her in one of my classes. We talked a lot between classes and in the library. I watched her become frustrated at class requirements; watched her as she grew in self-confidence. She, I'm sure, saw me going through similar things.

I didn't know, until she told me during our senior year, that some male students had accused her of talking too much with me. They had told her: "You should stay away from that White dude. Looks bad."

I'm grateful she didn't take their advice.

In my senior year, after Angela had given a report on racism in Christian Ethics class, everyone in the class except me, of course, discussed how it felt to enter a place where there were no other African Americans. They talked about Whites ignoring them, seeing them as non-entities.

I asked if they'd like to hear my opinion on the issue. They seemed surprised, apparently never thinking about my being the only White in the room.

The White professor explained that three years earlier there had been a group that had demanded that the Hood administration hire no more White professors. He also said that he had received anonymous hate mail in the past.

My classmates were shocked that racism had been shown toward the professor and me.

"The churches don't do enough to bring the races together," one of them said.

My response: "I'm not sure they really want to."

The professor disclosed: "I tried to become an AME Zion minister, but no bishop would talk with me."

Another classmate reacted: "I don't want to get into it, but there are certain things Blacks are going to maintain control over."

"I wholeheartedly agree," added a gentleman who was already a full-fledged minister in an African American church. "The White man has taken a lot of things away from us, but we're not going to give up our way of worship."

6. Subtle Racism

Sometimes racism directed at me was subtle. For example, we had daily chapel services led by students with guest preachers. It was always a good service and a welcomed interlude in a long day. One morning, about five minutes before chapel time, I was walking down a hallway when one of the upperclass students called out: "Hey, you. I don't know your name, but I want you to read the scripture for today."

He motioned for me to come toward him.

I kept walking, smiled, and said, "Sorry, not today."

Another example of subtle racism included a humorous aspect. It happened one afternoon in my Psychology of Religion class while we were discussing the phenomenon of child molestation.

One dear sweet lady (I mean that) made a statement, "No disrespect for Ron, but I've noticed that kind of terrible thing seems to happen more among White folk."

I chimed in, "Well, it's a well-known fact that 32.6% of all White males are pedophiles."

The professor rubbed his chin and said, "I don't know if those percentages hold true in the African American male population."

Brother T. looked at me, biting his lip to keep from laughing.

Waving my arms in the air, I said, "Hey guys, I'm just kidding. I made up that statistic."

Somebody asked, "What's a pedophile?"

7. A Different Culture

From what I have observed, male ministers are held in higher esteem in Black than in White churches. Perhaps that's because African American ministers, in years past, were more educated than the majority of their members.

Some of the customs that have developed for a male pastor in the Black culture include the following: he's asked to eat first at church dinners; he seems to be the only one able to bless the food; his wife is expected to sit on the front pew.

Visiting ministers in Black churches are usually asked to join the presiding minister and participate in church services. This is so entrenched in their culture that it is almost impossible to visit a church and sit with the congregation.

My initial experience with the latter custom happened with my homiletics professor. A man small in stature but with a well-built body, he boxed, worked out, and stayed in shape. He was a man of high intelligence, strong presence, and large ego.

His ego is what made him so good at what he did. He was excellent at beating "the five steps of a sermon idea" into our heads and immediately demonstrating the final product. After throwing out an idea, he would state the purpose of the sermon, then go to the text, to the hook, to the story, and be preaching it within a few minutes.

He was good.

One Sunday morning I attended his large-city AME Zion church. It was beautiful, obviously prosperous and active.

I arrived for the morning service, sat on the back pew, and waited for the service to begin. An usher asked me if I'd like to move closer to the front, telling me I'd be the only person back there.

Sheepishly, I followed him toward the front. Why worry about standing out in the crowd? Impossible not to do.

As the choir broke into song, the service leaders came through a side door and processed to the chancel. The professor saw me and nodded in recognition.

He motioned for an usher and whispered something in the man's ear.

The usher walked over to me and said: "The Reverend wants you to come up to the chancel."

"Me? Why?"

"Because you're a minister."

"But I'm not a minister. I'm one of his seminary students."

The usher left me and spoke to the professor again. He came back to say, "The Reverend said to 'Come up.'"

I went up.

The service was unfamiliar, but I followed the lead of an associate pastor.

The professor introduced me to the congregation by saying something like, "I'm glad to have one of my students who surprised me by coming here today. I expect that he's come to 'go to school' on me—to see if I practice what I teach." With a wide grin, he added, "Too bad I'm not preaching today."

He looked me in the eye and I got a little nervous. Thank God, he didn't ask me to preach or pray.

My learning process continued. I'd been unaware of the custom of inviting pastors to the pulpit and I learned years later that some Black ministers didn't realize this didn't happen in White churches.

One Black minister told me of a little White church he sometimes attended when he was not preaching at his own church. He spoke of how friendly everyone was. The spirit of love was evident in the manner the people treated him and his family. But he wasn't too sure about their pastor. He said, "The White man seems like a good guy, but he might be one of those who don't like Black folks in his church. He's never invited me up to the pulpit."

8. O. J. and Me
R. K. Journal Entry: 10-03-95

I left Hood this afternoon feeling disturbed, puzzled, and disgusted. The classroom building was still trembling from the cheers of O. J. supporters. Earlier, the verdict in his trial had been announced. Everything had come to a halt and the all-purpose room (the only one with a TV) was filled with students. When "not guilty" was announced, the room reverberated with laughter, clapping, hollering, and all manner of exaltations and "Praise the Lords!"

Seeing me at the doorway on the outside looking in, some of the revelers turned around and raised their clenched fists.

What did I represent to them?

The passive aggressiveness here is becoming tiresome. Why does everything have to be tainted by race?

Oh well, at least they are now open about it. Even the professor, who spends so much time convincing me that he is not a racist and sees color in everything, is able to be open with it in my presence, and that is as it should be.

But how can we improve relations between the races when the present attitude is held? How can the young lady be a minister of God's word when she openly says in class that she dislikes the fact that an African American preacher is a pastor in "the White man's church?"

The professor explained to her that it was okay because that particular denomination was anti-slavery during the Civil War.

I can honestly say that I have never experienced racism as I have during the last year at Hood.

A man whom I admire and look to for guidance told me not to hold back on giving leadership at Hood. From what I have observed, any leadership abilities I might have are not wanted; therefore, they have not been offered and will not be. I am positive that there is a certain faction at Hood that would be happy if Hood had never been opened to all who would come.

I have heard it said many times with pride that "Blacks" own Hood. I have seen how some of the African American professors talked about and acted toward White professors. I had thought it was a personality clash. Now, I'm not sure.

Here I am studying religion, trying to understand the Bible, and I find myself becoming disgruntled—or could it be I'm becoming prejudiced?

Last year I made an effort to socialize outside of class with classmates. I was put off, lied to, and some of the folks promised to get together with me later and never followed up. *So I don't try to socialize anymore. Most of my class-mates do not appear comfortable with me. I can understand that. I'm older and, thank God, I don't have to struggle to make ends meet like some of them do.*

I came here with the goal of attending class in order to study, to learn, to stay out of the way, and to just get along. My second semester I tried to expand as some professors had encouraged. It hasn't worked very well. I can get along with almost anyone. I have associated with all types and classes of people over the years. I can survive at Hood. If I desire to do more than just survive, I will have to make other decisions.

More today than at any other time in my life, I under-stand the plight of African Americans. And if I were in their shoes, I might be worse at taking out my anger on someone with a white face. Even so, there has to be a better way of blacks and whites living on the same planet ... and growing.

9. Pardon Me, My Anger's Showing
R. K. Journal Entry: 11-14-95

At school today I turned in my outline of the worship service (one of the course requirements for Dr. Moore's class). A Methodist district superintendent will be the speaker and I want it to be thematic. She gave me inform-ation so I can do that. I planned a simple United Methodist service with a Psalter and two hymns. I have a good team to work with. Things will go well. I went over the program outline with a staff member. Dr. Moore came to me with questions. I didn't put names on it and he thought I was doing it all. He made the point we should include as many students as possible.

After I explained the service to him, he said, "Okay, it looks all right."

I said, "Thanks, I'm too lazy to do the whole service."

Perhaps I should watch how I talk to him. He doesn't know me. He seems uncomfortable when I try to converse with him. Hopefully time will change that.

Looking forward to the service tomorrow morning. I feel good about it.

R. K. Journal Entry: 11-15-95

After my second class, I went to the office to get the bulletin for the service. The staff member didn't get it done yesterday, but this morning she told me she would have it ready in time. When I finally got to see the bulletin, it was not what I had prepared.

I'm a person who can control his actions, but I have never been able to hide my feelings. I was angry and then frustrated. I resolved to take what I had and make it work. The staff member explained to me that I had not arranged the service correctly. I had things out of sequence. She had left the Psalter in but rearranged it and added other parts of the service.

"Why?" I asked, but her explanation made no sense. This was at 10:15 a.m. and I had no time to find out where we went askew. I went to the library, sat at a desk in the

stacks, and prayed and studied and prepared myself and steamed.

The service went well, but I still didn't understand what went wrong. Back in the library after lunch, I noticed that the staff member who had prepared the bulletin seemed afraid of me. Two of her colleagues would not look at or speak to me.

After a lot of thought, I went to the staff member and asked her to stand up. I gave her a hug and told her if I seemed angry with her, I was sorry. She apparently took my actions as a sign of weakness and said that she knew I was mad at her. She proceeded to explain to me all the mistakes I had made on my program sheet.

I had put the district superintendent's name in the wrong place. I had not put the hymn of rededication at the proper place (even though I had not put one in it to start with). I tried again to explain the changes I had been attempting to make when she made an interesting comment: "The worship committee usually fills in the blanks for you."

"You're telling me that I cannot change the outline of the program?" I asked. "That it should be the same for every service and I have no right to change it?"

"Yes, basically that's the way it is."

How inconsiderate of me to have the audacity to impose something different at Hood! The solidly entrenched method of worship has sufficed since 1879. Why in the world should I think a change, no matter how small, could possibly improve anything? How dare I try such a thing!

I had carefully planned the service, choosing hymns to fit the theme. I had selected the proper people to conduct it. Professor Moore had said it looked good, but I forgot the most important task—I didn't get that particular staff member's approval.

How stupid of me! I see my mistake. I was working under the mistaken idea that the worship service could be altered; that services used by other church bodies could add to diversity at Hood.

How careless of me! For a while, I completely forgot where I was. I forgot my place.

I'm beginning to understand how people can be consumed by inner anger.

"Come join us."

"Work with us."

"Be a part of us here."

The underlying message is, "Don't bring your own ideas or your ways."

"Know and remember where you are."

Just another day in the Hood.

The professor who required me to keep this journal wrote:

Ron,
This is not only so at Hood. When you go to a new church with new ideas, it will be the same!

R. K. Journal Entry: 11-16-95

Now I understand what caused all the trouble. One little piece of paper; one person who didn't hear; another who didn't work hard enough at explaining what he wanted; and another who appeared incapable of independent thinking.

The staff person is used to what she thinks should be the standard form of worship for Hood. Before I came along, she apparently took the information given to her by the student worship leader and when she filled in the blanks it came out a worship service. She tried to fill in the blanks for my service and they wouldn't fit. So she rearranged the service to fit her mold.

The staff member tried and succeeded in rearranging my ideas and putting them into her accepted form. She did an excellent job of it, too. It was, after all, a beautiful service. Of course, with the cast of players it would have been beautiful in any form.

Carry it forward.

I don't fit the form of what she expects. I must change.

This morning the professor who requires that I keep a journal passed me on the steps. I barely spoke to him.

"Are you all right?" he asked.

"We all have our ups and downs," I answered and kept walking.

I'm sorry I did that. I respect him very much. This is not his fault. Nor is it mine. Nor is it the staff person's fault. She is doing what she thinks is right. She believes she is following the rules.

Mistakes are acceptable as long as you learn from them and as long as you don't make the same ones over and over.

I have learned a lot from this mistake. I will not make it again. Alas, another person erred here and, sadly, she didn't see her error.

Now I lay this episode of my growth aside and prepare to continue forward.

I'm through with it. It's over.

A month later, after my professor had read this section of my journal, he noted:

Ron,

Thanks for allowing me the privilege to read this journal. I recall, though not in detail I read here, the situation with the service at chapel (11-16-95). From what I have gleaned, Zion has no set order of worship. Hence, it is not correct to call the way worship is usually done here, Zion's way. And even if Zion had some set order, worship in the seminary ought to and will reflect the richness of the denominational diversity of our community. [Name of staff member] was completely out of place to have changed your order of service.

10. Discrimination Is Not Always Racial
R. K. Journal Entry: 11-5-96

Members of my American Church History class had lunch together today: our White professor, two African American women (Ms. Allen and Ms. Berry) and me. We ate Chinese food. The women told of being treated badly by some male students at Hood. Ms. Allen had recently assisted the Dean in giving communion. Some fellows told her she should not have done so since she is not ordained.

I had often wondered why these two women were usually seen together and rarely with a group. Perhaps it was because they were both targets of gender discrimination.

The oppressed (male Blacks at Hood) had become the oppressors.

The women also told me that at their last conference meeting they were not ordained but were held out. In that conference some males had been ordained with no seminary training at all. No women were ordained that year. Their bishop had wanted to set up a special training for women before they could be ordained.

11. Leaving the Hood

"Did you ever detect racism while in seminary?" colleagues and friends have often asked me.

My answer is always, "Yes, but shown by only a few people who never got to know me, mostly upper-class students."

In my first year I had often felt as if I were being ignored and looked down upon. The second year was not as bad. And the third year was great. I felt accepted and didn't have to prove myself to anyone. I was surprised at graduation when I received the senior award for didactic preaching.

From what I have observed, when the oppressed segregate themselves in any place such as a social club, a church, or a seminary, and a member of the oppressor group enters, it seems inevitable that bigotry and racism will rear their ugly heads. However, this was evident in only a small minority of the student body at Hood. But that's the way it is in the world, isn't it?

The greater majority of Whites are not racists, but we sit quietly by as the minority commit acts that paint our entire race as oppressors.

If you were to ask the people I've mentioned in this section (regardless of the color of their skin) if they were racists or if they were prejudiced, their answer would probably be, "No."

We don't see the things that those who are slighted see. Some of my closest friends to this day are those I met in seminary. We have discussed this issue. None of them ever saw, ever recognized, what I saw as racism. Was I overly sensitive? Was I looking for what I expected? Does everyone? Why did they not see it? Was it because they never thought they could be racists?

The saddest part of it all is that some of them were already pastoring churches. What did it mean when they preached brotherly love to all? How could they proclaim Christ's love for *all* people when their actions said other things?

Fulfilling the Call

In the second part of her sermon, Dr. Weddington tells the story of how I *just happened* to be appointed to a cross-racial ministry a few weeks before I graduated from Hood.

Sermon
for
"Pastor Appreciation Sunday"
at
Philadelphia UMC
December 17, 2000
Ron Karriker, Pastor

(Part 2)

Then in the spring of 1996, the woman preacher retired.

A few days AFTER her retirement, she *just happened* to be at the church to pick up a few things and Ron *just happened* to come by for a few minutes.

And at that very moment, it *just happened* that the district superintendent came by to call on the new pastor.

Ron was introduced to the district superintendent; she learned of his background,
> that he was attending Hood,
> had one more year to graduation,
> and had an interest in a future pastoral appointment.

Did this *just happen*? One has to wonder.

The rest of the story you know.

While Ron was completing his final year in seminary, the pastor of the Scotts Chapel—Philadelphia charge, who was rapidly declining in health became disabled so that he had to retire, and
> YOU were praying for a pastor who would
> > preach the word,
> > love the people, and
> > stay with you for a while!

It *just happened* that there were no African American ministers available. So your district superintendent remembered the White man with the gray hair and beard who had made his way successfully through an all-Black seminary.

She looked at your need and Ron's potential and Ron Karriker became your pastor.

Can there be any doubt that God called Ron and prepared him specifically to be your pastor?

Look at all the major turns that occurred as a result of "a coincidence" —
OR was it the direct intervention of God?

The stirring and restlessness that made Ron leave his family church.
The woman preacher across the table at the reunion Ron NEVER attended.
Wanda needing a book that could be found ONLY at Hood Seminary.
The unplanned meeting of the woman preacher, Ron, and the district superintendent at the church in Mooresville.
And your former pastor being able to continue JUST LONG ENOUGH for Ron's preparation to be complete.

Coincidences? Never!

These events testify to the <u>hand of God</u> working
for the good of his people,
for Ron to fulfill his calling, the desire of his heart and
for your prayers to be answered.

And so it is that

Pastor Ron is here.
You know he loves you.
And you love him.
He preaches the true word of God.
He visits the shut-ins.
He visits those in the hospital.
He teaches Bible Study.
He sings in your choir.

He counsels with you when you need him.
He represents you in the community.
He takes part in joint services in different churches.
And you are PROUD OF HIM.

You and he together have forgotten all about racial
distinctions AND you are setting an example for all to see,
saying as Paul said to the Galatians:

"There is no longer Jew or Greek,
there is no long slave or free,
there is no longer male or female,
AND (we add) there is no longer BLACK or WHITE;
for all of us are ONE in Christ Jesus."

Yes, Ron Karriker was CALLED—
        No doubt about it!
        Called to be
                a preacher,
                a teacher,
                a pastor.
        Called specifically to Scotts Chapel and Philadelphia.

AND . . . he works hard for you and for your church.

You know he could move on to bigger churches and higher
salaries if he chose to, but his love for you keeps him here.

Yes, your pastor was called—

BUT preachers are not the only people God calls.

You, too, are called, every one of you.

Don't look at the person on your left.

Don't look at the person on your right to see whom I'm talking to.

I'm talking to YOU!

I repeat: YOU are called.

Hear how Paul puts it in his letter to the Corinthians:

"There are varieties of gifts, but the same Spirit; and there are varieties of service, but the same Lord; and there are varieties of activities, but it is the same God who activates all of them in everyone."

What did he say?
Everyone has gifts.

God ACTIVATES these gifts in—

JUST THE PREACHER?
JUST A FEW church leaders?

No.

God activates these gifts in EVERYONE so that his work can be done.

This is Pastor Appreciation Sunday.

I have been a pastor.
You probably guessed I am the woman preacher in Ron's story.
As a former pastor, would you like me to tell you the best possible way to show your appreciation for all this Man of God does for you and your church?

It's Christmastime.

What gift could you give him to show your love?

    Words of thanks are good.

    Expressions of love are good.

    Gifts on occasion are great.

But what your pastor needs most, what would thrill his heart above any other gift is your fervent and energetic support in the work he is attempting for God in this place.

Gleanings From the Promised Land

In her sermon, Dr. Weddington used an analogy that strains my humility. She compared my quest to that of Abraham's journey to the Promised Land. I'll have to concede, however, that after I received God's call, I did "set out not knowing where I was going" as did Abraham.

I'd often prayed "for a little church out in the country or I guess I could handle a little church in the city." And I ended up with one of each: Philadelphia in Stony Point, North Carolina and Scotts Chapel in Statesville, North Carolina.

In this section I share with you some of the best as well as some of worst experiences in this segment of my life's journey as a White pastor in a cross-racial ministry in the United Methodist Church (UMC).

1. The Sun Rises
"Could you preach for us this morning?"

A woman from Philadelphia greeted me when I pulled into the parking lot before sunrise on Easter morning, 1997. I'm not sure how she knew who I was except maybe she thought I was the White preacher that had been appointed to come to her church when their pastor retired.

Almost frantically, she continued: "I'm the lay leader and our preacher got real sick yesterday and couldn't make it this morning."

"Thank you for your confidence in me," I responded, "but it would be wrong for me to take over before he retires."

Earlier in the week I had spent parts of two days riding around with the elderly retiring pastor of the Scotts Chapel—Philadelphia Charge. He spoke about the churches and their members. He truly loved them, but because of poor health he knew he could no longer stand the grind and strain of being their pastor.

I did a lot more listening than talking, as I am a believer in learning from my elders, gleaning bits and pieces of information, hoping to avoid mistakes. He had invited me to attend the joint Easter Sunrise Service at Philadelphia.

I opened the car door and stepped out to be greeted with the aroma that only an early country morning on dairy farms can give. For some reason the lay leader seemed embarrassed by my having to endure the odor, but I assured her it only made me feel at home.

As the sky was getting light in the east, the worshipers walked to the edge of the cemetery.

The service began.

Under the direction of the lay leader, we sang a few Easter hymns and she asked me to pray.

After my prayer, when I looked across the tombstones, I saw the sun making its presence known by bringing its light into our world, just as the risen Christ had done that first Easter morning.

It was a good day. We ate breakfast prepared by the men and talked of days past and days to come.

I was surprised when two women told me that they were grandchildren of slaves, because I had never realized how close I was to living in that tragic time in our country's history.

One of the women related that her grandfather had been freed when he was nine years old. He was known as a "pet" around the plantation since he got to live in the master's house. This woman treasures her grandfather's shaving mug that has been handed down through her family.

The week after Easter my district superintendent called and asked me if I could preach on Sundays until I was officially appointed pastor.

Later I learned more about the history of both churches. Scotts Chapel (at a different location and with a different name) was established in 1885. The congregation moved to the current location in 1905 and changed its name to Scotts Chapel, honoring a Mr. Scott who had donated lumber for the building.

According to a history published in the 116th Anniversary Booklet (2001), I was the 46th minister to serve the church. Twenty pastors had served a year; 24, two to six years; one, 12 years. I was to serve seven years.

I learned that members of Philadelphia had paid for their original church building with the proceeds from selling cotton grown on land that had been deeded to the church by a White landowner. The men of the church had plowed the ground and planted the cotton. The women had hoed the cotton while their small children played on quilts within eyesight of their mothers.

The landowner had stipulated in the deed that if the church ever ceased to exist, the land and buildings on it would revert to his heirs. Imagine what would be required today to divide that small parcel among hundreds of heirs.

One day I walked through the cemetery of the White Presbyterian church about a half-mile down the road. Tombstones at both churches carried many of the same surnames. When I got to know the people at Philadelphia well, several talked about being descendants of some of the early White members of that Presbyterian church.

I met a few members of the Presbyterian church who admitted kinship with Philadelphia members. Every now and then one prominent landowner from the Presbyterian church would show up for funerals at Philadelphia.

2. A Special Day

On my first Sunday as an appointed pastor, I arrived at Scotts Chapel at 9:15 a.m., 45 minutes before the service was to begin. It was ironic that I would be working in the same area of town where I had worked for the Welfare Department in the 1960s. The neighborhood looked about the same as it had three decades earlier.

Three women were holding Sunday School in the sanctuary. I went into a room off to the left side of the nave that looked like it could have been an office at one time. I put on my robe. At 9:55 a.m., I walked into the chancel where the women were ending their Sunday School class.

In front of the altar, I prayed a brief prayer. As I sat down in the pastor's chair, I felt a mild panic.

What's happening? I wondered. *Is nobody else going to show up?*

At 10:00 a.m., the choir members came in and took their seats. The lay leader entered through the right side door and stood at the lectern. As he was making announcements and beginning the worship service, a few people began to arrive and take their

seats; however, almost all of the pews were still emp-
ty when it came time for the ushers to take up the
offering. After some more singing and by the time I
began my sermon, the church was almost full.

Hmm, I thought as I looked out at all the late ar-
rivals. *Perhaps I'll need to change the order of worship a
little. Can't run a church without the money.*

Turned out to be a very good, inspirational service that ended at eleven o'clock. Lots of people had
come to see the White preacher and I was hoping
they'd all return the following Sunday.

Getting to Philadelphia (13 miles from Scotts
Chapel) on time for the 11:30 service was tight. When
I arrived, the parking lot was full and cars were
parked on the shoulder of the road.

"Hey, this is great," I smiled at Wanda. "All these
people coming to meet me as their new pastor."

A black sedan pulled up next to the sidewalk
leading to the front doors. The car's back door opened
and out stepped the now retired former pastor. He
waved to me and smiled. I met him at the bottom of
the steps, gave him a brotherly hug, and followed him
and his wife into the sanctuary. They went up to the
first pew and sat down. I went into the pastor's office.

The lay leader came in to see if I needed anything.
On a prior visit to the church, I had asked this woman
about their plans for honoring their former pastor's
service. She'd said they wanted to give him a special

day. That was a good thing to do. I had encouraged them to do it but requested: "Please have that done before I officially become your pastor."

Although I felt that the day should be special to this man, I also felt that it should be special to me.

"Why is your former pastor here?" I asked.

"He's been ill and this is the first time he could come to church, " she explained. "This is the first day we could honor and say good-bye to him. A lot of his family and friends are here."

What was I to do? This aged and ill man of God had come to one of the churches he had served. He was probably expecting something special, and here I was without a clue as to what to do.

I put on my robe.

Things change when you put on your robe. Things that seemed hard become easier. Your persona changes. You become the pastor, the preacher, the one in charge, the one with the answer to the question.

Confidently, I walked into the sanctuary and invited the guest to come up into the chancel with me. I offered him my seat directly behind the pulpit. He refused but took the chair next to mine—a gracious gentleman till the end.

The service began. I welcomed everyone, including the retired pastor. Although I offered him the pulpit, he stood where he was and thanked the congregation for his special day.

The sermon went well. I referred to the guest several times. He seemed to enjoy what I was saying, as he became quite animated, frequently shouting, "Amen!"

After the service he told me my sermon was the best he'd ever heard. He was being gracious, I know. No matter how good you are, better can be found, and I wasn't that good.

I thanked him and shook his hand. Side by side we walked to the back of the church. When everyone had said their good-byes, one of his family members escorted the retired pastor to his car.

As they drove away, I knew I was watching a man who had given his life and his health working among God's children, spreading the good news to all who would listen.

Now, as it happens to us all, his time was up. I hoped the day was special for him. It was for me. After all, how many ministers have had the distinction of preaching at the retirement services for their predecessors?

3. Differences Celebrated

I remember well those first days as a White pastor in a cross-racial ministry: the tiptoeing around cultural issues, the differences in customs, and the freedom demonstrated in African American worshiping styles.

It was not unusual for someone to break into song after I had prayed, or to respond to sermon points with loud "Amens," or to participate in altar calls at the end of the service. All new customs to me, they quickly became part of my worship style.

Getting into the service brought about a spiritual reality that had been unknown to me. But now I anticipated, sought after, and looked forward to such experiences. Personal testimonies of what God had done and vocalizing what God was doing in individual lives opened my mind to how worship could be.

As the Sundays passed, the settling-in process became less stressful. We became more comfortable with each other, the members and I.

4. The First Lady

"How's it feel to be the First Lady?" my best friend from seminary, Brother T., asked Wanda one night when we were visiting with him and his family.

Thinking he was teasing her, Wanda laughed. Neither of us had ever before heard that term used as a synonym for the preacher's wife.

Wanda understood what he had been talking about the next Sunday when she went with me to Philadelphia.

We entered the church: I, through my outside office door; she, through the front door. Two ladies wearing black skirts, white blouses, and white gloves ushered. One of them grabbed Wanda by her arm and led her down to the front pew.

I said "grabbed" and that's what happened. This woman was well known for her strength and endurance. She was tall, muscular, and strong and always the first person asked to help on cleanup day. Wanda had resisted, I'm told, but she was the First Lady and she quickly learned that First Ladies are supposed to sit on the front row in this church.

So down front my dear wife sat.

After church Wanda explained to the ushers that she didn't feel comfortable sitting at the front and would rather sit further back. The ushers never pushed her again, but let her know they had been acting from tradition.

Another tradition changed suddenly and without any comment after Wanda's appearance at the church. She wore pants when all the other women wore dresses. The next Sunday we noticed that several women were wearing pants. I guess some changes in tradition are easier or more desirable than others.

Although respectful of the African American tradition of calling ministers' wives, "First Ladies," Wanda has always been her own person. My mission as a minister was never hers; however, she has always supported my work. She is a Ph. D. level psychologist who, since retiring from private practice, has continued to advocate for survivors of extreme abuse through writing and international research on this phenomenon. She is author of the novel, *Morning,*

Come Quickly, a story in which she shares what she has learned personally and professionally about the aftereffects of extreme child abuse and the resiliency of the human spirit.

And, of course, she's my best friend.

5. Why Am I Here? (Part 1)

At ninety-one, Jake was one of the first people I visited in my role as a Reverend. (In the African American churches with which I am familiar, clergy persons are usually addressed as Reverend or Rev rather than Pastor.) We sat on the front porch of the local fertilizer and farm supply store where he worked.

The clapboard building, which was about the same age as Jake, had a small office that led into the warehouse or stock area. Inside the office was a small wood stove that people sat by to keep warm in the winter when cold air blew through the cracks in the walls. The window was opaque from years of dirt, soot, and grime. Old wooden straight-back chairs with cane bottoms awaited the next occupants. A platform out front was high off the ground to facilitate loading. An old wooden bench, with Coca-Cola printed across the back, sat on the front porch.

The store was a wonderful place. A place where hardworking, independent, and opinionated people came to share conversations with friends. The color of one's skin did not keep one and all from gathering.

We talked about Jake's job that included opening the store and selling fertilizers, seeds, lime, and assorted supplies. He told me about his wife, Miss Maggie, who lived in a nursing home. And we talked about a lot of get-acquainted, mundane things.

The next time I visited Jake was at his modest home. He greeted me at the back door, took me through the den and down the hallway into his formal living room.

After chatting for several moments, he suddenly became quiet. He stared at his Duo-Therm oil heater as if he were trying to come up with the right words to say what he wanted to say.

Finally, without looking at me, he spoke: "I've been wondering. Why would God send us a White preacher?"

Again he became silent as if sorting out the things he wanted to add, so I waited quietly.

Gazing out the window, he answered his own question: "I believe God has a purpose, something you're to do here."

"Do you know what it is I'm supposed to accomplish?"

"Nope, but I'm thinking on it."

"Well, sir. When you figure it out will you let me know?"

Jake looked at me over his wire-rimmed glasses. Grinning, he answered, "Yes, I will."

6. Confusion at the Nursing Home

Miss Maggie, Jake's wife, lived in a skilled nursing home. An aide informed me that I could find her in the dining room. The slim lady with slightly stooped shoulders was easy to spot—she was the only person in the room.

I walked over and extended my hand.

"Good morning Miss Maggie, I'm Rev Ron, your new pastor."

She ignored me.

I tried again. This time a little louder.

"Good morning Miss Maggie, I'm Rev Ron, your new pastor."

She looked over the top of my head, squeezed her eyes shut for a few seconds, opened them, and stared at me. She glanced from my white face to my white arms and back to my face.

"You ain't *my* preacher!" she said.

Perhaps she couldn't understand how I could be a minister since I was not wearing a coat and tie. (I usually wore comfortable slacks and short-sleeved knit shirts when I was working.)

"Who *is* your preacher?" I asked.

She mumbled something that I couldn't understand to which I responded: "Your preacher became ill and had to retire. I'm your preacher now. I'll be visiting you and bringing you communion if that would be okay."

I handed her my business card. She read aloud the names Philadelphia and Scotts Chapel.

"I live in a church," she said, pointing to a group of residents in the hallway. "Church just let out."

For a few minutes we talked about other things that made little sense. Finally I asked, "Could we have a word of prayer together?"

She nodded.

We prayed.

Standing up to leave, I extended my hand again. "Miss Maggie, I'm Rev Ron, your new preacher. I'll be here for you if you need me."

She reached for my hand.

I left wondering if the woman would even remember me after I went out the door.

7. Not Wanted: White Preacher

During that first summer at Philadelphia, I learned more of their church history. It involved previous community days led by church members, preaching and worship services under the arbor, dinner on the grounds, horseshoe games, and softball tournaments.

Longstanding traditions included yearly revivals held in August with an African American Baptist church about a mile down the road. It went like this: Philadelphia's revival began on a Sunday afternoon when the Baptists would travel to Philadelphia and be treated to a covered-dish dinner prepared by the Methodists. In mid afternoon the Baptist minister,

Reverend Turner, would start the weeklong revival by preaching the sermon. Guest preachers would conduct services for the next five evenings. At the end of Philadelphia's revival, the Baptists would begin their revival at the next Sunday morning service with Philadelphia's minister preaching the sermon.

This tradition had been honored for about a century and continued when I became pastor at Philadelphia, but not without some major problems.

A hint of discord came when it was my turn to launch the Baptist revival. Reverend Turner and I had entered the chancel and were standing in front of the congregation when a late-arriving couple rushed through the double doors at the back of the church and glanced toward Reverend Turner and me. They quickly turned around and walked back out the doors.

At the wrong church, I surmised.

During the service, Reverend Turner ended his introduction of me with, "If Philadelphia can accept him, we can too."

I knew I was in trouble, but at the time had no idea that the congregation's reaction to the first White preacher to ever stand in their pulpit would have been so cold.

Several times while preaching, I glanced at the elected elders, all men, who sat on the second pew glaring up at me in the elevated pulpit. It was their pew, their place of honor, their place to monitor what was happening to ensure that the Gospel was preached.

Sitting directly behind me, Reverend Turner seemed to be pleased with the sermon. I could hear his quiet, encouraging "Amens" and sense his involvement in the spiritual nature of the service.

Not so for the elders.

Making a collective statement they sat stoically, staring at me, their lips tightly closed, most with arms across their chests.

None laughed at my attempts at humor.

No "Amens," as I had become accustomed to hearing in the Black churches. And if I didn't get them, I wondered if I were getting my points across.

Near the celebration point of the service, Reverend Turner whispered: "Have an altar call. Have an altar call."

So I announced an altar call. Though not my first, it was by every measure imaginable, the strangest. In the invitation, I talked about the saving grace of God, of God's love for us, of Jesus dying on the cross for our sins, and of accepting God's offer of salvation.

Nothing happened.

Nothing.

The elders remained in their pew obviously intent on teaching me a lesson. I turned around and glanced at Reverend Turner.

No help.

I looked toward the cross on the altar.

No help.

Undoubtedly God had confidence that I would endure and grow in faith during this learning experience.

I talked, preached, almost begged for what seemed like an eternity, until at last I saw movement toward the back of the sanctuary. A lady stood up, worked her way to the main aisle and walked toward the altar rail.

MY WIFE – THE FIRST LADY!

God had sent me help years ago. After all the praying, all the talking, all the cajoling, the one to come forward was the only other White face in the congregation.

As Wanda knelt at the rail, women from Philadelphia who were in the choir rose and joined her.

Then several women from the congregation.

Then men from the choir and some of the men from Philadelphia.

It was beginning to get crowded down front.

The elders? They looked uncomfortable. Looked at each other with questioning glances until they, too, howsoever reluctantly, came to the rail. I felt no great outpouring of love and spiritual blessings, but it was a start.

8. A Second Chance

Five evenings after my poor start at the Baptist revival, Philadelphia's choir provided music for their closing night. As was customary, I, as Philadelphia's pastor, participated in the service by offering prayer and reading scripture. Prior to the service, I had met the preacher of the night in Reverend Turner's study.

Reverend Lewis, a middle-aged man, sat on the sofa with an artificial leg on his lap, working on a shoe. Diabetes had taken one leg and losing the other was a real possibility. He had a shunt in his neck for kidney dialysis, and his doctors had suggested he give up preaching.

"I'll quit when the Lord takes me home," he said.

He looked at his watch and came to his foot. He offered his hand and I took it in mine. Then he pulled me close and gave me a brotherly hug.

I had never met the man before, but after this brief encounter I felt as if I had known him forever.

The service began. Introductions were made. I read scripture. The choir sang a few moving gospel hymns and my newfound friend began to preach.

He preached hard that night, the same message I had preached five days earlier. But there was a big difference.

People became more involved.

Elders in the second pew were on their feet more than seated.

"Amens" were heard everywhere.

At the close of Reverend Lewis' sermon, he offered the invitation for an altar call. Seemed like everyone in the building ran over each other to get to the rail with the elders being first to get up there and kneel down.

What was the difference? I had also preached hard on the previous Sunday morning. I had prayed for goodness in the listeners' lives. I had talked of God's grace and God's gift of salvation. What was the difference?

When all who could come were at the rail, Reverend Lewis turned to me and in front of God and all present gave me a hug and said: "Brother, go pray for the people. They need your prayers."

"Are you sure," I asked.

"Yes, I'm sure. They need your prayers."

All of those elders at the foot of the pulpit, looking up for prayer from the White preacher.

Another example of God's sense of humor.

9. Ken and the KKK

It was a little disconcerting when I learned that, a week before my arrival at Philadelphia, the local branch of the Ku Klux Klan had marched in a neighboring town.

Later I asked Ken (Gleaning #20) what he thought about the KKK.

"Oh! They're just a bunch of good ol' boys who don't have anything else to do. Doesn't mean anything. I know a lot of them and, if I was in need of money, I could ask a few of them for a hundred dollars, and they would bring it to me. They're all right. Don't cause any trouble."

I had hoped the KKK would not cause me trouble in the future. After all, I was a White man preaching in a Black church in their community.

10. Phantom of the Florist

I love flowers. Anything that grows, brings color, and has a pleasant aroma gives me the feeling that the world is not all bad. Flowers do that for me. Real flowers. The kind you water and put in the sunlight.

Not artificial, but real flowers.

You can imagine how I felt upon arriving at church one Sunday morning to see plastic flowers all over the place: on the altar, in the windows, on top of the piano. They were so big they overshadowed the cross. We almost had to part the hardened fronds to see it.

Now I'm a follower of Hoyt L. Hickman. He wrote a book (no best seller I'm sure) titled *United Methodist Altars: A Guide for the Congregation* (Revised Edition, 1996). Every church should have this book. Every member of the Altar Guild should have access to it and read it.

On pages 62-64, Hickman provides a list of rules regarding flowers in the church. He writes:

> 4. Do not place flowers on the Lord's table, as this practice detracts from the primary purpose of the table as the place where Holy Communion is celebrated.
> . . .
> 7. Flowers symbolize the resurrection, and in keeping with the principle of integrity, no type of artificial flower or plant is appropriate to the environment of worship.

I noticed artificial flowers on the altar one Thursday when I went into the sanctuary to practice my sermon for Sunday.

I moved them to the top of the piano.

Saturday they were back on the altar.

I moved them to the top of the piano.

On Sunday morning they were back on the altar.

I moved them to the top of the piano.

This went on and on for several weeks. The phantom florist was as persistent as I.

On Thanksgiving Day I walked into the sanctuary to see a new arrangement on the altar—a huge cornucopia flowing with plastic fruits nestled in plastic autumn leaves.

Beautiful in someone's eyes.

But for the altar?

I moved the cornucopia to the top of the piano. Saturday it adorned the altar. I moved it back to the piano.

On Sunday morning I walked into the sanctuary and turned toward the altar.

Where's the cornucopia? I wondered.

I found it on top of the piano.

The next Sunday it was gone.

Who WAS that phantom florist?

11. Mountain Dew Surprise

"What can I do to get people to come to church?" is a question every pastor probably asks when thinking about growing the church.

"What would make the people in the community want to come to my churches?" I asked myself. Some likely came the first Sunday just to see the new White preacher.

They came; they saw; they left, never to be seen again.

As I sat on the front steps of Scotts Chapel one afternoon, I looked at the houses up and down the street. After being there a few weeks, I had met some of my neighbors when they were out walking. I'm sure most of the ones I'd not met knew about me. But how could I get to know them?

I had been walking the sidewalks speaking to every person I saw, but to become known as part of the community, I needed to do more.

What about Mr. Quick? (No, he's not a fast man.) It's a convenience store on Depot Hill. I'd been told it was a place I didn't want to be after dark.

Well, there are a lot of places I don't want to be after dark. I don't want to be in the woods after dark. Don't want to be walking on dark streets after dark. Don't want to be anywhere I'm not wanted before or after dark.

The folks on Depot Hill, so I was told, didn't like White guys like me hanging around. But surely it would be okay if I went there in the daytime, wouldn't it?

The next day, I ventured up to Depot Hill around lunchtime. I wanted to get to know the manager of Mr. Quick. I got out of my truck, walked to the door, and looked inside. The place was packed. I didn't know that in addition to selling groceries and beer and cigarettes, they also served a hot lunch at noon.

I took a deep breath, opened the door. Seemed like everybody in the place was talking at the same time. Loud, boisterous, happy. I stepped inside.

Everything got quiet.

I walked to the back where the coolers were, opened the glass door, and reached for a Diet Mountain Dew. I turned to go back up front to the cashier when I heard a loud voice:

"Hey, Rev Ron."

I turned around and saw Joe, one of my members from Philadelphia. I walked over to him and we shook hands.

"Hey, everybody. This is my new preacher, Rev Ron."

That bit of information must have sounded okay to the packed house.

Someone shouted, "Hey, Rev."

Somebody else said, "Good to meet ya, Rev," and everyone went back to doing whatever they had been doing.

Question: What are the odds of my going to a strange place and running into one of my church members who introduces me to that lunchtime community?

I had been a little nervous, but they made me welcome in their own way. I had prayed for guidance from above and I found a surprise here below.

By the way, the Mountain Dew was on the house.

12. Change is Scary

Statesville is a typical southern city with friendly, hardworking, God-loving people. It's also a city struggling with the need and desire to bring everyone together. At least that's what the public relations people would have you believe.

Could be true, but history doesn't die easily. It's still a city divided by a railroad track and economical and social tracks as well.

Like I said, it's a normal southern city.
Thoughts and opinions are difficult to change.

Soon after becoming the White pastor at the Black
church, I received a letter addressed to:

Pastor, Scotts Chapel United Methodist Church

It was a reminder of the monthly meeting of the
Black Ministers' Association. Statesville has always
had two ministerial associations—one "White" and
one "Black."

I suppose there are a lot of reasons why this is so.

Change is a frightening thing to some people. If
the two associations were to come together, old
customs would have to change. Fewer leaders and
more followers would be necessary.

From what I had heard, disagreement over where
to hold the city's annual Easter Sunrise Community
Service had always prevented attempts to bring the
two associations together. It had always been at the
White cemetery. The Black ministers felt it should be
held every other year at the Black one.

So two services continued. After all, how could
they be sure Christ would rise in the *other* cemetery?

Christ died for us all—Black and White, old and
young, Southside and Northside. Yet we can't get
along well enough to celebrate the one act in our
Christian faith that sets us apart from other religions.

God came to earth in the form of his son to die on a cross and to rise from the tomb on the third day, and we bicker about where to celebrate this most wonderful occasion.

How sad.

Can we change?

I attended the meeting. Some of my brothers in Christ were uneasy. One was an alumnus of Hood and a friend. I explained to him that I'd received the notice and felt that perhaps the name of their association should be changed to "The Ministers of Black Churches Association."

One of the leaders of the group looked at me, smiled, and to my surprise said: "I've watched you work among our people while you've been here. You're Black enough to be part of this group."

Later, a funny thing happened. They lost Scotts Chapel's mailing address. At least I think so, since I never received notice of another meeting of the Black Ministers' Association.

13. My Office (That Wasn't an Office)

Every church should have a Mr. Williams on the roll. Two would be great. Soon after my arrival the elderly man, a Korean War veteran, came to visit me in my office (that wasn't an office) at Scotts Chapel.

We talked about the church building, the people, the history, and the reasons for their not getting things they needed that had been planned long ago: stained-glass windows, a new steeple, a new sign in front of the building and, most of all, a pastor's office.

I quickly learned that the small church was always struggling to pay its bills. It took until December to get enough money to pay the conference dues. Little money was left for upkeep.

I talked with Mr. Williams about my office (that wasn't an office), a small room on the front left side of the sanctuary. The walls, ten-feet high, were built of concrete blocks that needed a paint job. The room had one window and three doors: a door to the sanctuary, a door that led directly to the pulpit, and a door to the outside. It lacked heat, air conditioning, carpet, and bookshelves. An old desk with a dilapidated chair sat in the middle of the room. No pictures hung on the walls.

One morning when I arrived for work, Mr. Williams was painting the room with bright yellow paint. He'd missed a few spots, and I thought about coming in one evening and giving it a second coat, but Wanda cautioned, "That's his contribution. Leave it alone."

And I did.

Later he installed a small window air conditioner. What a difference that made!

Now to get some heat.

The resourceful man came up with an old gas heater that could be hung on the wall. He and a friend brought the heater over and made it ready to install.

They drilled some holes through the wall to run copper pipes through to connect with a gas tank outside.

He suggested, "Rev Ron. Maybe you should go do some visitations. Or go home. Or go up to Philadelphia church. Go somewhere."

I wouldn't budge, so he informed me that the heater had been stored in an area where animals had frequented, and he didn't want me around when he put fire to it.

The man appeared embarrassed, and I probably should've listened to him and left, but I stayed. He turned on the gas, lit the pilot light, and gave it the gas.

Man, it stank!

But as Mr. Williams had said would happen, the odor burned off. He aired out the room, leaving only traces of the smell of burnt urine.

With heat, air, and newly painted walls, he had made the room a place for a real office.

14. Two of Jesus

After the pastor's office at Scotts Chapel had been fixed up with a new coat of paint, heat and air conditioning, a bookcase, and new carpet, I noticed the walls were bare. What could I use to decorate them? I rummaged around and found a picture of Jesus in a storage room. It was one where Jesus had light skin and hair, almost blue eyes, and European facial features. I thought about where Jesus was born, where he lived. For one who is native to that part of the world, the face didn't fit. Jesus' skin would have been dark.

Here I am, I reflected, *a pastor of two Black congregations. The picture of Jesus needs to be authentic. What can I do?*

Then I remembered another picture.

While I was in seminary and doing an internship at a White Methodist church, the sad plight of an elderly Black lady was brought to the attention of the men of the church. She lived alone in a rundown shack with no relatives to turn to and barely getting by—if her lifestyle could be called getting by. Her biggest problem was a leaky roof that was well past being useful. The men replaced her roof on a Saturday morning.

She was thrilled.

Thanking the men profusely, she presented them with a gift, explaining, "It's the only thing I have to give you."

The men graciously accepted her picture of a Black Jesus. They took it back to their church and gave it to the pastor who placed it, for safe-keeping, in the back of a closet that was rarely used.

All these years later, the picture had come to my mind.

I wondered if it was still there.

I went to the church and asked the pastor about the picture. We looked for it. There it was, in the back of the seldom-opened closet, covered with dust and waiting to come out. The pastor was glad to give it to me, especially after I told him I planned to hang it on my office wall.

Bring it out of the closet.

Hang it in public.

Let the people see it.

And see it they did.

I would ask people as they came into the office, "Which picture of Jesus is more authentic? Which do you like best?"

The European Jesus won every time. The Black Jesus wasn't accepted at all.

I guess we all get used to things as we have always seen them. My church members had never seen a Black Jesus.

I wonder if it still hangs on the wall or if it has been put in the back of a closet somewhere and forgotten?

Too Black!

15. They Left Me Alone

After I had been at Scotts Chapel awhile, attendance increased, bringing in more money to fund needed projects. With some new furnishings, including a custom-built bookcase and a new desk chair, the office (that wasn't an office) had become a place for me to be easily available for members of my congregation and the community.

A couple members suggested I not stay in my office after dark.

Remember, this was the neighborhood where I was told not to go after dark when I had worked there as a social worker three decades earlier.

Funny, I never feared being in that office at anytime day or night, a sacred place in the middle of a neighborhood where drug dealing was openly observed on the streets. Everyone must have known that the White guy driving the 1992 calypso-green Ford Ranger was a preacher and that they should leave him alone.

And they did.

16. Stereotypes

Soon after the Scotts Chapel office had been revamped, the men of the church scheduled a workday to clean up the building and grounds and make needed repairs. As chair of the trustees, Mr. Williams planned it and called everyone into action. More men and women than I had expected came to do the work.

At one point I was helping tie up wires and yelled, "Somebody, give me a knife."

Nobody responded.

"Please, I need a knife."

Nobody responded.

"Listen, I know all you guys carry knives. I need a knife."

We all stopped what we were doing and looked at one another. There was not a knife among us.

"I thought all you guys carry knives," I pointed out again, this time grinning.

Wiping sweat off his brow, the church lay leader explained: "Hey, we were taught all you White guys carry knives."

After some good laughs about our stereotypical ideas, we went back to work.

17. My New Supervisor

One day Mr. Williams came to the church carrying his toolbox. He brought in painted boards to repair a hole in the bathroom wall. The hole was about a foot above the floor, making it necessary for him to lie down to fix the problem.

He asked for my help in measuring the area that had to be covered. I took the tape, lay on the floor, and following Mr. Williams' instructions, marked where nails were needed. He cut the wood to the correct length, handed it to me, and pushed a hammer my way.

For about 30 minutes I worked on my hands and knees in that tight space between the sink and the commode. After finishing the job, I stood up, stretched, and looked for Mr. Williams, seeking to get his approval.

I didn't have to go far. He was sitting in the bathroom doorway in a comfortable chair supervising my work.

"Looks good," he said.

"But Mr. Williams," I said. "If I remember correctly, my job description says nothing about my having to do carpentry work."

18. A Lesson in Proper Etiquette

Early in my cross-racial ministry, not knowing correct protocols caused me embarrassment and humiliation. At Hood, no one ever taught me the proper etiquette when going into another pastor's church to help with services.

One of my members had asked if I would assist in her father-in-law's funeral. I eagerly agreed, not only to help this grieving woman, but also to get to know other pastors. I wanted people in the area to know who I was, instead of just being that "White preacher" up at Stony Point.

Thirty minutes before the service, I arrived at the church and went to the pastor's study. He was seated behind his desk writing. I extended my hand and called him by his name, but he didn't answer.

Was I at the wrong church?

I looked at the bulletin my member had given me where my name was listed as assisting minister. Turns out I was at the right place, but under the wrong circumstances. And it was my fault for allowing myself to be drawn into a situation where I had not been invited.

Finally I engaged the pastor in conversation, but he never stood up to leave the safety of his desk. He hardly raised his eyes to meet mine. I felt a little like I did when, as a kid, I was caught doing something I should not be doing, but was not sure what it was I should not be doing.

"What do you want me to do in the service?" I asked.

"Whatever you wanna do."

At that moment, I wasn't prepared to do what I would have liked to do.

Suddenly everything became clear.

I should not have accepted the invitation from my church member to assist in the funeral. The pastor should have been the one to invite me. I had embarrassed the pastor and myself. What if he had not wanted me there? The decision had been taken out of his hands.

The pastor glimpsed up at me a few times from his position of ignoring me and I offered an apology: "Reverend, I now see where I have handled this improperly. You and not anyone else should have invited me. Please accept my apology for such a breach in etiquette. I'm new at this, but common sense should have told me better. Sir, this is your service. If you don't want me to be part of it, say so, and I'll be on my way. I have other things I need to be doing. In fact, I'll go. I hope it'll take some pressure off you."

"Take a seat," he said, then proceeded to explain the service, tell me what scripture to read, and what time to be ready to enter the sanctuary.

The time came and I joined him and three other ministers, one a woman. Five of us entered together. I was last in line behind the woman. I wondered about the seating arrangements but wasn't concerned, knowing we would all be seated.

Five chairs were lined up behind the pulpit. The other three men sat in high-backed, padded chairs. The woman sat in a less comfortable-looking chair. I sat on a metal, folding chair that leaned to the left and was harder than the floor.

I told myself that they didn't plan it to turn out this way. Just happened. Luck of the draw. But deep down, I wondered.

I leaned over and spoke to the woman.

She ignored me.

Well . . . she probably didn't hear me above the organ music.

A little later I spoke to her again. No reply. No glance my way. No smile. In fact she looked stern.

Well . . . funerals are serious matters. Best to concentrate and ignore the man sitting next to you, I presumed.

My time came to read scripture and the pastor introduced me. As I walked toward the pulpit, he stopped me and whispered in my ear: "After the scripture, have the prayer."

This would be the prayer for the family that is supposed to calm them, soothe their pain, and give them hope for the future and a guarantee of eternal life.

Earlier in the morning, as I stepped into the shower, I was thinking about death. Washing my hair, I reflected on how God makes a way where there seems to be none; how God gave the last sacrifice ever needed so we might have everlasting life. It's God's gift being handed to us and, like any gift, we have to reach for it and take it before we know what the gift brings. If we receive the gift, then we should act accordingly.

Those thoughts in the shower had given me my afternoon prayer.

The service ended. The deceased's family and friends walked slowly to the grave plot. The other pastors paid their respects to the home pastor and left. I followed suit, thanking the pastor for his patience and for including me. I turned to leave, and he stopped me, asking, "Will you go with me to the graveside and participate in the interment service?"

I nodded. He gave me a book, showed me what parts to read, and we joined the procession. After the service was over, I said "Good-bye" and left.

Lesson learned: When working with a pastor, never impose your nose where it may or may not be wanted. Use common sense and wait to be invited to participate.

19. A Touch of Fate

About five weeks after the funeral where I had learned a lesson in proper etiquette, one of the saints from Philadelphia passed away. The family wanted a nice quiet funeral—nothing elaborate.

On the day of the funeral, as I sat in my office prior to the service, the unexpected happened.

I heard a knock at the door.

"Come in," I said.

Guess who it was?

In walked the woman pastor who had snubbed me at the last funeral where we had both participated. She had a big smile on her face, apparently believing she was where she should be . . . and then she recognized me.

Five weeks earlier she would not even speak to me. Here she stood prepared to offer her ministerial expertise. Her eyes got big; her smile quickly faded away. Her posture slumped as she stood before the one she had refused to acknowledge at the previous funeral.

I jumped to my feet, rushed to shake her hand, and welcomed her to my church. I escorted her to a comfortable chair, introduced her to the other pastor, and told her how happy I was to see her. I instructed them both about their parts in the funeral.

At the appointed time we had a prayer then walked into the sanctuary. I pointed to a chair for her to use.

It wasn't a metal folding chair.

It wasn't leaning to one side.

It wasn't cold and hard.

It was my chair.

She took the chair and smiled.

Remember the old saying about heaping coals of kindness upon the heads of those who have wronged you? She received a heaping head full of love and thankfulness. I treated her as a friend—respectfully. She appeared happy that I had made her a part of my life.

Over the years our paths crossed again in hospitals and at other churches. Never again did she refuse to treat me as a friend.

20. Advanced Lesson in Patriotism: 9-11

How long will it be before the numbers, 9-11, will no longer be tinged with blood, hatred, and memories of fear? How long will it take to smile again when they are mentioned? Another generation? Two?

I remember it well. I was in my office at Scotts Chapel when the phone rang. "Rev, are you listening to the news?" It was our lay leader speaking.

"No, Willie, I'm working on a sermon. Why?"

He told me about all that was happening in our country. Of the horror of airplanes hitting buildings, of thousands of people dying.

"I thought you might want to get in touch with Wanda," he said. "I bet she knows."

I called my wife. She had been getting her car serviced when she saw the first attack on television. We talked for a while. After I hung up the phone, I walked into the sanctuary, up to the altar, fell on my knees, and cried. I could do nothing else. Later I prayed. Had a conversation with God. Well, maybe it wasn't a conversation because that takes two.

That day I did the talking. I asked the questions. Questions to which there were no answers. How can people hate so deeply? It's not possible, is it? Why Lord? Why?

I received no immediate answers. I was left alone to think of how everyone's life would be changed forever, of how a new generation would have learned a reason to perpetuate the hate and the evil that caused such things to happen.

Then I thought of the following Sunday's service. *What do you say? How can you explain any of it? Sunday's sermon is there on my desk, but it's nothing compared to the hurt and confusion that will be in my congregation. I'll just pray and wait. Wait till Sunday. Wait for the questions to come. Wait for the tears to flow. Wait for God's guidance.*

This is way above my pay grade.

Sunday came.

When it was time for the sermon at Scotts Chapel, I stepped into the pulpit, held up my notes, and threw them on the chair beside me.

We talked. No preaching. No more service. We talked. I'll never forget how the congregation expressed their feelings. Some had been in WWII; some in the Korean War; some in Vietnam. Some currently had children in the service.

All worrying: "What will happen now?" Old men cried. Young, usually boisterous children, remained quiet. Women wiped their eyes. And we talked. Then we prayed. We prayed a lot.

Cries such as these need answers, but there were none. So we talked and we prayed some more.

When the service was over, and I stood at the back door greeting and comforting people, a young lad, maybe five or six, with fear and puzzlement on his face, tugged at my robe, asking, "Rev Ron, am I going to die?"

I bent down to his level, put my arms around him and tried to comfort him. "No child, no. You're not going to die. You're okay and safe here at home."

That has always been true. We were safe in our town and in our home. Was it still true this day? The world had changed. Driving to my other church, all I could think of was the young lad's question: "Rev Ron. Am I going to die?"

The Philadelphia congregation was subdued when I entered the sanctuary. During the sermon time, as I had done at Scotts Chapel, I opened the floor for discussion about the attack on our country. Response was about the same. People shared their sorrows and their concerns with each other and with the entire congregation.

Murmuring ceased when Ken stood up to speak (Gleaning #20). In the Air Force for almost 30 years, he had reached the highest grade for an enlisted man. His job was to keep large cargo planes flying, and he had done that in various conflicts all over the world.

Tears ran down his cheeks as he spoke of his love for his homeland and his hope for the future. When he sat down, the entire church remained silent until I called for prayer.

At both churches, pride in our country had been shown by words and actions.

What was left from the discussion for each person present was a personal resolve that terrorism against America would not change how we live and think.

We would live, but would also remember.

How could we not?

The news media urged Americans to ring community and church bells on the following Friday at 12:00 noon to honor 9-11 victims. Scotts Chapel had a big bell in the churchyard that hadn't been rung in many years because the clapper had no rope. I went to a hardware store and bought a piece of rope and attached it to the bell.

On the appointed day at the appointed hour, Wanda and I put our hands on the rope and through our tears rang the church bell.

21. Stutterer at the Carwash

Who would ever think individual philosophies of life would be highlighted at a carwash?

One Saturday morning I drove to the carwash, pulled in line, instructed the attendant about my car's needs, paid the bill, and went inside to await the emergence of a clean car.

I enjoy talking with people, having discovered that most people, no matter the gender or race, will react to a kind smile, as did the lady in front of me who was having her black Mercedes washed. Probably in her mid seventies, nicely dressed, she was articulate.

As we talked, I learned that she had been at the beach and had come to get the salt residue removed from her car. She laughed as we discussed nothing of any importance. Two sociable people enjoying communicating with each other.

During our conversation, I mentioned that I am a Methodist minister and said, "Last Wednesday at Bible Study, a few church members picked at me because my car was dirty, shaming me into bringing it here."

"What church do you serve?"

"Two churches. Scotts Chapel here in Statesville and Philadelphia in Stony Point."

She thought for a moment. "Would you repeat those names again?"

"Scotts Chapel and Philadelphia."

The expression on her face changed to disbelief. "Scotts Chapel? Isn't that a . . . uh . . . isn't that a Bl-Bl . . . isn't that a Black church?"

"Yes, they both are. And some of the most God-fearing, God-loving people I've ever met."

"And you like that?"

"Why yes, I do. I'm starting my fifth year there. God has truly been good to me."

Three times, she'd tried before she could say the word, "Black." Apparently she was unable to get past the fact that although the color of my skin was the same as hers, I served two Bl-Bl-Black congregations.

The strange look on her face suggested uncertainty, unbelief, and absolute disgust.

Her car rolled by on the other side of the viewing area and out onto the pavement. She stood by the window, her back toward me, watching as the attendant dried if off.

What is she thinking? I wondered.

She never faced me again; never spoke to me again; never smiled again.

As I contemplated what had just transpired, I remembered Jesus' answer (as recorded in the tenth chapter of Luke) to the lawyer who had asked, "And who is my neighbor?"

Jesus answered with the "Parable of the Good Samaritan." To the lawyer, the idea of a good Samaritan would have been an oxymoron. When Jesus asked him who treated the man who had been robbed most neighborly, the lawyer could not even spit the "S" word out of his mouth, but answered, "He that showed mercy."

The woman at the carwash had to force herself to say the word "Black," slamming shut the door to further communication when faced with a reality that didn't fit her "White" world.

Such a nice person—a person who could have so much to offer if her worldview was not clouded by racism and prejudice.

So much wasted.

So much never realized.

So many opportunities lost.

I left the place with a sparkling clean car but a heavy heart. In my mind, I could hear Jesus and the lawyer talking:

"Who is my neighbor?"

"He that showed mercy."

"Go and do likewise."

22. Sympathy at the DMV

My driver's license was due to be renewed so one day I stopped by the Department of Motor Vehicles (DMV). This was out in the country and must have been a lonely place, because when I arrived no one was there except the examiner. I told her I needed a renewal and had stopped by to get a booklet to prepare for the exam.

She smiled. "Oh, you don't need to study. Sit down and let's try it."

I took the test, having no problem at all. As I stood up to leave, she asked, "What do you do for a living?"

"I'm a United Methodist minister."

She leaned across the table, making close eye contact and said, "I joined a Methodist church in town a couple years ago, but it was so cliquish I could never get to know anyone. I moved to a Baptist church. I'm happy there. Where do you preach?"

"I have a two-church charge: Scotts Chapel in Statesville and Philadelphia in Stony Point."

"I've never heard of either one," she said.

I wanted to say, "You have to have contact with something before you can recognize it," but refrained and said: "Both are African American churches."

She sat back in her chair, putting more space between us, and asked in an almost sympathetic tone: "Why did they *do* that to you?"

23. The Beautiful; The Ugly

Weddings are blessed occasions. Everyone gets involved and is happy. So it was when one of our young ladies announced her forthcoming marriage.

Right away I recognized a problem. Not enough room. Large family on both sides, lots of friends. Our little church would not accommodate the expected crowd.

The bride-to-be considered having the wedding in another church. She called a large downtown White church, told its administrative assistant her situation, and asked if she could use their church.

"Yes, by all means. Non-members often hold their weddings here."

Problem solved.

Or so I thought!

Three days later the woman from the downtown White church called back saying, "I talked with the pastor and he said there is a conflict, the church is not available for that date."

Hmm?

The bride found another church—this time a Black church in a neighboring town. I had met its pastor, Reverend Wright.

No unknowns about this church.

Or so I thought!

The wedding went smoothly, everything on time —a great wedding day for a beautiful bride and groom.

As the guests left, I made my way back to the pastor's office just in time to see a woman standing close to the pastor and shouting: "What was that White man doing up there in that wedding? Why were you not there? He had no business there." She was 'in his face,' animated, angry, and ugly.

Reverend Wright calmly replied, "He was there because he's the young lady's pastor. Let me introduce you to him . . . since he's standing right behind you."

She whirled around and looked at me. Without speaking she stormed out of his office.

"Hope I haven't caused you any trouble with this congregation," I said to my pastor friend.

His answer has stayed with me until this day, and I'm sure it will forever. "If you and I can't do what we know to be right, then who can?"

Within a few months, this humble, soft-spoken, man was voted out as pastor of the church.

All for doing what he knew was right.

24. A Separation of Church and Hate

Our district of the UMC owns a camp in the North Carolina mountains—a lovely setting for worship, retreats, outdoor sports, hiking, etc. with an inviting swimming pool.

One summer, I called to reserve the camp for my churches to hold a joint Sunday morning service in the main building and use the other recreational facilities in the afternoon. The camp director told me the building was available for us on the day I requested, but that a group of young people from a large White church in a nearby city had also scheduled to use the pool in the afternoon.

"That'll be fine," I had said, having no idea our being there would present a problem to anyone, especially since the director said we could split the cost of hiring a lifeguard for the afternoon.

As Wanda and I drove onto the campground, we noticed a group down by the creek. I assumed they were the young people with whom we'd be sharing the pool.

After a brief worship service, we enjoyed a picnic lunch. The meal went fast. Couldn't take too long because the horseshoe pits beckoned the older men. The women headed to the building where old-timey wooden rocking chairs lined the long porch—perfect for rocking the tiniest church members and catching up on the latest happenings in both church communities.

The pool waved with the warm mountain breeze, inviting our kids to come dive into its cool waters. They hustled to the bathhouse, put on their bathing suits, and ran up the dirt path to the pool where the lifeguard was already in his chair. A few of the teenagers dived into the deep end. The younger ones went gingerly down the steps to the shallow water. As usual, the big kids looked after the little ones.

Where's the White group from the city church? I wondered. *What if they saw our Black kids in the pool and went home? Oh my God! I hope I'm wrong.*

An hour later no White kids had ventured into the pool.

Too crowded?

Chemicals out of balance?

Too cool?

Driving out of the camp, Wanda and I saw the White group still hanging out by the creek. Further on down the road we met the camp director walking toward the main camp. I stopped and opened my window. We chatted for a few moments. I told her how much our group had enjoyed the day and asked, "What happened to the other group who was supposed to share the pool with us?"

"Oh, they were here," she said. "They decided not to go swimming."

Then, as if she were unaware what she had done was wrong, she admitted she had called the church's youth leaders the week before to let them know that a group from two African American churches would be sharing the pool with them.

Apparently the White group had chosen to stay down by the creek while the Black group enjoyed the pool.

Lots of fun in that, I know. Catching crawfish and frogs. Getting their shoes wet. Staying to themselves and feeling safe. Didn't have to meet anyone new. Didn't need to learn to communicate with and understand people different from themselves.

25. The Kente Stole

February is Black History Month and in our churches we used this as an opportunity to teach the people, especially the children, about things and people in the Black culture for which they can be proud.

I always had a brief children's sermon each Sunday so the teaching of Black history fell upon me —sort of like a frog teaching a kangaroo to jump. The kids were always way out in front of me.

One Sunday, I decided to use my Kente stole to explain the history of the cloth. Lots of books and articles are written about Kente cloth, its origin and meaning. In preparing for the children's sermon, I learned that Kente cloth is part of the philosophy and culture of the Ashanti tribe dating back to the 17th century. Originally it was only used for royalty. As more cloth became available, the price came down and others were able to buy it. The different weaves in

Kente cloth mean different things and are marvelous to see.

Armed with this vast knowledge of Kente cloth and holding my Kente stole, I, as was my custom for children's sermons, called out, "Come on down!" And the children came running down to the front of the sanctuary. I sat on the step leading to the altar and the children sat in a semicircle around me.

I proudly held up my stole. "See this. Do you know what I have here and what it means?"

An adorable little girl about five years old raised her hand, waved it in the air, and said loud enough for everyone in the congregation to hear, "I know, I know. It's some more of that Mexican stuff!"

So much for the children's lesson in history and culture. But this old White fellow had learned a lot.

26. A Tenderhearted Man
R. K. Journal Entry: 07-10-97

Visited the Ruckers today. Mr. Rucker said he likes the Book of Job. In our conversation about Job, he said: "Job prayed for his enemies."

"Do you have enemies, Mr. Rucker?" I asked.

"We all do," he answered.

"Do you pray for them" I asked.

"Yes. It pays to do so just like Job did."

Who would have dreamed I would become one of those enemies Mr. Rucker had talked about on my initial visit with him and his wife. It had to do with a misunderstanding between Mrs. Rucker and some of the members of the church over a community event.

I went to their house to tell them how her position looked to those on the outside of their reasoning, including me.

The aging gentleman came to the door, received me warmly, and invited me into his home. He called his wife to come into their living room. We talked about their children and grandchildren, how their garden was growing, and other things they were interested in.

After several minutes I broached the topic of a conflict Mrs. Rucker had with some of our church leaders.

To my surprise (and I'm now surprised it was a surprise) the man, visibly distraught, shouted: "Just because you're a White man, you think you can come into my house and talk to me and my wife like that?"

I was the Man—the projection in his eyes for all White men who had wronged him and his people.

Dumbfounded at his accusation, I sat back in the chair, my mind devoid of any response. How do you respond to such a statement?

At last I looked him in the eye and said: "Sir, you invited me into your house and if you wish me to leave I will do so immediately."

The man responded by springing from his chair and stomping out of the room.

Apologizing for her husband's remarks, Mrs. Rucker said softly: "He didn't mean what he said. He's just tenderhearted."

Oh, he meant what he said and he is anything but a tenderhearted man, I thought.

Mrs. Rucker did not offer to try to resolve the conflict.

I excused myself and left.

Later, at a called meeting of the church council, I relayed what had taken place in the Rucker's home. Several group members smiled at the story as if they had known what would happen if I confronted Mrs. Rucker about her handling of the community event.

The council decided to ask Mrs. Rucker to appear before them to discuss the situation, to which she agreed.

At the meeting, she listened closely to their concerns and asked, "Did I do wrong?"

After much discussion Mrs. Rucker admitted fault in the way she had carried out the community event.

What did I, as her pastor, learn from this experience?

Number one: I learned that I shouldn't let the church council use me as a shield to hide behind so they can deny their own responsibilities.

Number two: I learned that *tenderhearted*, in the way Mrs. Rucker used it to defend her husband, obviously meant something different than the traditional meaning in the White culture of "having a kind, gentle, or sentimental nature."

Sometime after I had met with the Ruckers, I came across the following passage in Maya Angelou's *I Know Why the Caged Bird Sings*:

> Then, too, I was well known for being "tenderhearted." Southern Negroes used that term to mean sensitive and tended to look upon a person with that affliction as being a little sick or in delicate health. So I was not so much forgiven as I was understood.

When I asked a member of my congregation what the term *tenderhearted* meant to her, she told me that in her culture, the word is used to describe a person who is having emotional problems.

Number three: I learned that as a White pastor in an African American church, I was an easy target on which a man could project his unresolved anger toward the White race.

How long had Mr. Rucker's feelings toward the White man been just below the surface of his being? Who or what did I represent to him on that particular day? He was a proud man, a property owner. He had run his own business. He seemed to be respected by both Blacks and Whites.

Yet, in this community it had been only a few decades earlier that Blacks were allowed to work in the local mills and poultry processing plant. Previously, they had been relegated to farmwork, housework, and other jobs that profited the White man and kept Black men and women in servants' roles.

This couple's grandparents had been slaves.

How long does it take to allow the wounds to heal?

How long must the Black outwork, outthink, outperform, and outlast the White man before those not so ancient scars are no longer apparent?

How long?

Will they ever go away?

I forgave Mrs. Rucker for her action and understood where Mr. Rucker was coming from when he attacked me for being White.

When I next saw the couple, they acted as if nothing had happened between us and remained active and supportive members of the church.

It's sad what we go through sometimes to learn what is true—true of others and true of ourselves.

As Job had forgiven his enemies, I trust that Mr. Rucker had forgiven his enemy . . .

Me.

27. I Just Can't Get It Right

The United Methodist Church is continually seeking ways to aid in the growth and improvement of its pastors. One of those ways is the yearly evaluation of church staff members by the Pastor/Parish Relations (PPR) Committee. In a pastor's evaluation, such things as preaching, visiting, and teaching are judged.

Toward the end of one such evaluation of me, the chairperson stated: "Your preaching is getting better. You visit. Your Bible studies are very informative. Overall you're doing an excellent job. But Rev, there's one thing we all think you need to work on."

"What's that?" I asked. I couldn't recall anything I had done that had not already been addressed.

The chairperson continued: "Well, we think that when you sing with the choir, you need to improve on your swaying from one foot to the other and clapping your hands on the offbeat."

He demonstrated by moving to the beat of an imaginary spiritual to show me how it should be done. Everybody in the room laughed at his insinuation that I, along with all White folk, "Ain't got no rhythm!"

What did I learn from this evaluation?

I learned that humor goes a long way in diffusing reactions to our different cultural practices.

28. The Chambers Street Gang

On late afternoons I would often sit on the front steps of Scotts Chapel. I always spoke to anyone who walked by and would sometimes walk down the street to let my neighbors know I was around.

One afternoon a group of children (five boys about nine to twelve years old and one girl about nine that I had noticed hanging out together and walking the streets) came over to the steps and struck up a conversation with me. Previously they had ignored my attempts to be friendly.

They asked me who I was and what I was doing there. After several more questions, they finally asked if they could go inside and get water. Any excuse, I suspected, to gain entrance to a place they had never seen. I invited them into the church, showed them the water fountain, and watched as they began to roam around the building.

In subsequent days the church became their oasis, their place to stop for a drink of water. One evening they came in when we were having choir practice. I handed a mike to the oldest child, the leader of the gang.

He stood on the steps of the chancel and sang some song while the rest of us watched. He was a complete ham and enjoyed the stage. The kids left and choir practice resumed with what seemed like a better feeling of brotherhood and sisterhood than before the children came.

The next day I noticed something missing from the back pew: the long lighter acolytes use to light the wick of the candle lighter. I immediately knew who had taken it. The only child to pick it up and examine it. The leader of the group.

Next evening as I sat on the steps thinking how I should deal with the theft, the gang came back. This time they brought two older boys with them. They tagged along behind, which was unusual for this crowd—14 and 15-year-old boys being led by a 12 year old. Not in this neighborhood!

The leader walked confidently up the steps, stopped in front of me, and almost demanded entrance to get some water.

"Not today," I said.

"What do you mean?" he asked, obviously upset that I was challenging him. "Why not?"

I answered with the authority that some people expect from the clergy: "Last evening you stole something from the church. You can come back in when you've returned it and not before."

Oh, he was at a loss. He was the leader but could not lead. Entrance to the church so he could bring the "big boys" in was being denied.

"I didn't take nothin'. He pointed to the young girl. "If something's gone, she took it."

So far the two older boys had kept their mouths shut. Now one entered the conversation. "What'd he take?"

I described the long lighter. The older boy's next question was the teller.

"What color was it?"

"Green. About six inches long," I answered.

The older boy jabbed his index finger onto the leader's chest and threatened: "Man, donchu know you don't steal from the church?"

The gang left and never returned. I often saw them at night prowling the 'hood.' Apparently their parents or caregivers were working or didn't care where they were, so they cared for themselves— learning all the 'proper' ways to act.

Do what you want to do, but whatever you do, don't steal from the church.

Sad.

29. The Insurance Man Cometh

Too bad the kids discussed above didn't have Miss Sadie as their neighbor. I had met this lovely lady when I made my first round of visiting disabled church members who couldn't attend church.

I knocked on the front screen door. She answered, squinting her eyes trying to see who I was.

"Are you the insurance man?" she asked.

I laughed and said, "Well it depends on how you look at it, I'm your pastor."

She laughed with me.

Years later I visited Miss Sadie when she was in the hospital because of heart problems. On the way to her room, I met a family member who told me that Miss Sadie had suffered another heart attack about an hour before my arrival and was in the intensive care area.

I went to Miss Sadie, held her hand, read a few verses of scripture, and prayed. Suddenly, she grasped my hand, sat up in bed . . . and died.

Miss Sadie was the first person I had ever seen die. At her funeral, I used a story her daughter had told me about her mother.

One summer day the daughter had come home from work to find children from the neighborhood on her mother's porch, in the house, in the yard, everywhere. But that was not unusual, because her mother loved children and children loved Miss Sadie.

Her mother was standing on the porch plaiting a child's hair.

The daughter asked, "Mom, who is that little girl? I don't know her."

"I have no idea who she is."

"Then why are you fixing her hair?"

"Because it needs fixin'." And Miss Sadie kept right on plaiting.

That was Miss Sadie. Someone who would jump into the middle of things just because they needed fixin'. How odd a behavior in

—a time when we don't always know our neighbors two houses down the street;

—a time when the feeling of community for many folks is held inside their own four walls;

—a time when helping a neighbor's child could bring a letter from a lawyer.

How many people in today's world jump into something just because it needs fixin'?

30. Happy Birthday and Good-bye

Fred was a good man, one of the best. Married with two daughters, two sons-in-law, and three grandchildren, he was a hard worker and had been employed by the same company for many years. He was a member of a large extended family—the type of family that lived out the true meaning of the word "family." They were close. Fred and several of his family were members of Scotts Chapel. Some of his extended family were members of the House of Prayer for All People.

Fred seemed to have it made, but he had prostate cancer. Treatment had kept it under control for 20 years, but in his early sixties, it began to suck the life force from his body. He suffered many stays in the hospital only to improve, go home, go back to work, and eventually back to the hospital.

Fred turned 65 years old during his last stay in the hospital. None of his close family members had ever reached 65.

Wanda and I went to a birthday party held for Fred in the hospital's recreation room. A room full of Fred's family and friends celebrated with all kinds of remembrances, including having his grandchildren sing the songs Fred liked.

I don't remember exactly what was happening at the time, but all of a sudden Wanda and I realized this was more than a celebration of attaining 65 years of life, it was also a celebration of what could be called a "homegoing" for Fred.

We all knew, as did Fred, that he was dying and would not be with us much longer.

Fred was going home to the God he loved and followed—going home to be with those who had gone before.

They brought out the cake. Fred wheeled his chair over to the table to help light the candles. We all sang "Happy Birthday." He blew out the candles.

And the alarms went off.

What had happened?

Someone pointed to a smoke detector directly over the cake. Hospital employees poured into the room. Firemen showed up within a few minutes.

Fred died a few days after his birthday party, a couple days past his 65th birthday. I was with him and his close family when he died.

A good man going home.

31. Standing in the House of Prayer for All People

"Rev Ron, I don't want any big funeral and I want the funeral to be held in my church." Before he became critically ill, Fred and I had discussed how he wanted his funeral.

Scotts Chapel seated approximately 150 people. I estimated the number that would come to Fred's funeral would be far more, yet, I remembered his request and would honor it.

Or so I thought!

While I was contemplating what to do, the phone rang. It was the pastor for The House of Prayer for All People. We had met before and were not total strangers. He began talking about Fred's funeral and reminded me that many of Fred's extended family were his church members.

Then he said something that surprised me.

"I want to offer you and the family something I've never done before, Rev Ron. You can use my church for the funeral. Have whatever kind of service you wish. Have a Methodist service. It won't matter. I'll be at the funeral to make sure everything goes well for you and I'll keep the band under control."

(The band included drums, trumpets, trombones, and tambourines. They loved to play and would play for long periods of time without stopping. They were great.)

The pastor reiterated: "Rev Ron, this has not been done in this church before." Meaning, a White man had never preached from his pulpit.

I was stunned. What an offer, especially being made to me. I was torn between what Fred had requested and what would be needed to satisfy the crowd that would surely come. Fred's wife and daughters wanted to use the House of Prayer and we did.

The church was full for Fred's funeral. I was told it would hold around 300 people in the pews.

The family entered and filled up one side and about a dozen pews on the other side. Friends filled in the remaining pews, and I don't know how many people were standing outside.

A testimony to Fred.

As we say in the South: "Anyone who was anyone was there." The congregation included politicians, city leaders, and the local president of the National Association for the Advancement of Colored People (NAACP).

We sang a lot of songs. Fred's grandchildren sang his favorite one. It was obvious the band was not liking this part of the service. They were not playing, and they were becoming restless.

We used a traditional Methodist service and it went well. When I said, "Amen," and announced the service would be continued at a cemetery in town, the band exploded. They were still playing when we left the church.

It was a great day, celebrating the life and death of a good man. God was worshiped and praised and White and Black people came together for the good of all.

32. Why Am I Here? (Part 2)

"Why would God send us a White preacher?" Mr. Jake had asked when I first visited him (Gleaning #5). He had no answer at the time. Neither did I. He had promised to let me know as soon as he received an answer.

About a month before he died at 96 years of age, I visited him in his home and asked: "Jake, have you figured out why God sent you a White preacher yet?"

"Well sir. I believe he sent you here to get my granddaughter back in church."

I had met his granddaughter, Linda, when I was visiting Jake and she had come by to see him after she got off work one day. I learned that she was married, a mother and grandmother, and worked in the lab at a local industry. Jake had told me she had grown up in church but had strayed away. He had wanted very much to see her back in church.

Over time, I had noticed her coming in to church just as the service began. She sat in the back, showing little participation in the service and always leaving before the service was over. I never had an opportunity to speak with her on Sundays.

I spoke with her about this when we were visiting her grandfather at the same time. She told me: "I'm not sure why I come at all."

As time passed, Linda became more visible in the church. She began to attend regularly and joined the choir. At the time, we didn't have a pianist. She honed up the piano skills she'd learned as a child by practicing on the church piano during her lunch hour. She began playing for church services.

On a later visit Jake told me he had never ceased praying for Linda's return to church. He believed my coming as his pastor was a sign from God that his prayers were being answered.

I visited him one Sunday after he was placed in a nursing home. He lay in bed, smiling, looking upward, and waving at persons only he could see. He sang a few hymns and I followed along as best I could. After a brief prayer I left and went home.

My phone was ringing as I walked through the door. It was Linda.

"Pop just died," she said.

This beloved man left this earthly world with a smile on his face and his granddaughter at his side.

In her strong voice Linda sang at his funeral.

Was I really sent there to help her find her way back to church? I don't know for sure. I do know I learned much from our association. Probably more than she had learned.

33. Revival Time (Revisited)

The tradition of Philadelphia's holding yearly revivals with the Baptists down the road continued throughout my tenure with Philadelphia. Many friendships came out of those revivals. Friendships and understanding, but for a long time, the uneasiness of having a White man in their pulpit continued.

Five or six years after that first revival (Gleaning #7), I learned that prior to my initial appearance in their pulpit, some of the elders had pushed for cessation of sharing revival time with Philadelphia.

It failed.

One of their church members told me he had pleaded with the elders: "Give the man a chance."

On my last revival opening, I stood in their pulpit and recalled my initial sermon with them. The atmosphere was much warmer now. Not as much suspicion, more acceptance. Seven years had made a big difference in both the Baptists and myself.

After greetings all around I asked, "Do you remember the first time I preached in this pulpit?" I could see heads nodding, hear laughter and a few "yeses" coming from the congregation. "Well, I was really uncomfortable. Were you?"

More nods and laugher. Perhaps they were non-verbal admissions that they had been insensitive to me in that moment. A few of the usually stoic elders who guarded the purity of the sanctuary nodded in agreement.

I preached that day, more comfortable than ever before.

I had my last altar call in their church.

I was leaving the community, but those dear Baptists down the road would always be in my memory. What a loss that would have been if the tradition had ended because I'm White.

34. An Asinine Question

The District Committee on Ordained Ministry plays an important part in the supervision of local pastors. This committee is made up of a representative from the Board of Ordained Ministry, the district superintendent, and at least six other clergy in the district.

Since I had made the decision while in seminary to remain a local pastor, I was required to meet with this committee each year. Each year there were new members. Each year I had to explain my work and why I remained a local pastor.

At one such meeting I, wearing a suit and tie, walked in to meet the group. My colleague, a senior elder among the African American ministers in my district, took one look at me and said, "Well, we got him dressing like a Black preacher."

"Yes sir," I replied, "all I need now is a Cadillac."

I had learned that a Black minister at the meeting had recently bought a Cadillac. We all enjoyed the levity of the moment.

Then I was asked to tell those who didn't know me about my education, background, and cross-racial appointment.

A White minister asked: "You're the pastor of an African American congregation? (To this day I can't remember this man's name and I don't ever remember seeing him again.)

I explained my coming to these churches right out of seminary. His next question must have shocked everyone in the room. "Do you think you could preach at a White church?"

He was dead serious.

Now what in the world was he thinking? What would make him ask such an asinine question? Especially in an integrated committee that included three African American elders.

Did he believe that I was an inferior pastor who had been placed in African American churches because I wasn't intelligent enough to preach in a White church?

Or perhaps his view of Black preaching always included screaming and hollering and jumping over pews or some crazy assumption. Anyway you look at it, I perceived it as a putdown of Black pastors and churches, and me.

I looked at my Black colleagues. One was my district superintendent, a man who was staring at the floor as if he were embarrassed—probably for me and also for the man who asked that question. Another sat with tightly closed eyes with an expression on his face that made him look like he had bitten into something that was distasteful. The third looked puzzled, as if he were saying, "What did he just say?"

No one in the room made a sound.

Finally, smiling at the questioner, I answered, tongue-in-cheek (or was it?): "I'm not sure if I could lower myself to do that or not."

I waited for the laughter, but all I heard was . . . more silence.

35. Moving On

Seven years after having been appointed to the cross-racial charge, I realized I needed a change and my congregations needed something that I couldn't give them.

For the previous two years I had asked to be moved. On each occasion the district superintendent had a place for me, but everything fell through in cabinet meetings with the bishop. My superintendent never explained why, but I always guessed it was because I was a local pastor and they had elders who needed places to go.

Each year some of the members of the District Committee on Ordained Ministry urged me to become ordained so I would be guaranteed a job. My answer was always the same: "When the Lord is through with me I'll go home."

Maybe this was the time.

Getting into the ministry at such a late date, I never thought I had the time to do what it took to become ordained.

So maybe the Lord was through with me.

I sent the district superintendent a letter of retirement effective June 30, 2004.

Retirement?

1. Angel of the Shoes

A few days after I retired, I received a call at around 2:30 a.m. from a former church member telling me that her husband had just died. She wanted me to do his funeral. Had to get the arrangements tended to immediately, I suppose. I might not have been available at 8:00 a.m.

I explained that I could not come back because she had a pastor and he was very capable of conducting the funeral. Anyway, her new pastor would have to invite me back. It's the proper ethics of the situation.

She thanked me and hung up her phone.

I went back to bed.

Within a few minutes my phone rang again. This time it was her new pastor. We talked and laughed about our having to conduct this conversation at three in the morning. He had no problem with my doing the eulogy for this man.

On the afternoon of the funeral, I arrived at the church, paid my respects to all present, and went to the office to prepare for the service. I put on my robe, straightened the accessories, and looked at my shoes to see if I needed to wipe the dust off them. After all when one wears a robe, all people see are his head, hands, and shoes.

I panicked. I was wearing old, old shoes—a pair of beat-up loafers that I should have thrown away long ago.

What was I to do?

I washed them; I wiped them with a wet paper towel; I brushed them with my hands. But nothing hides years of abusing your shoes. They looked horrible. I was embarrassed.

There was nothing I could do except overwhelm the congregation with my preaching so they would fail to look at my shoes. I said a prayer, sat down at the desk, and tried to control my emotions.

A young man, Jay, came into my office to see if I needed anything. I pointed to my shoes.

More serious than he had to be, he asked, "What size do you wear?"

"10-D," I answered.

"No problem. Exactly my size." He slipped off his shined-up shoes and scooted them over to me. I gave him my beat-up shoes to wear to the funeral.

After all these years, it still amazes me how God remains so steadfastly in control of whatever the situation might be. Now there are those who might not believe the Almighty would waste time looking after shoes. They could be right, but I do believe the Almighty looks after the folks who wear them.

The service went off without any problems.

Wonder if anyone noticed I was wearing a new pair of shoes?

Wonder if anyone noticed the donor was wearing a pair of shoes that looked like they should be tossed into the dumpster?

Leaving the cemetery I passed Jay and said loud enough for a crowd to hear: "Good lookin' shoes you have there my friend."

Jay will forever be my "Angel of the Shoes."

2. Back in the Pulpit Again

A couple weeks into my retirement, the district superintendent called and asked if I would fill in at two African American churches for an undetermined time.

For several years those churches had grown under the leadership of a pastor they had come to dearly love. He was a good preacher, a good pastor, and a leader with vision.

As it always happens in this line of work, the pastor left. They were happy for him but sad for themselves. How would they ever get someone as talented as this man?

Under the guidance of the superintendent, a man just beginning his seminary education agreed to be their new minister. All was in order for a good transition.

Or so they thought!

On the Saturday before the Sunday the new minister was to come, he had called to say he could not accept the appointment. I could only imagine what that did to those two congregations.

I looked for ideas about how to write a sermon for those traumatized churches and remembered one written by the Reverend Fred B. Craddock, a member of the Disciples of Christ denomination and a seminary professor. I had attended some of his preaching seminars.

The sermon is published in his book, *The Cherry Log Sermons*, with the title: "While the Minister Is in Jail." The text is from a letter Paul wrote to the young church at Philippi while he was in jail.

> [21]For to me, living is Christ and dying is gain. [22]If I am to live in the flesh, that means fruitful labor for me; and I do not know which I prefer. [23]I am hard pressed between the two: my desire is to depart and be with Christ, for that is far better; [24]but to remain in the flesh is more necessary for you. [25]Since I am convinced of this, I know that I

will remain and continue with all of you for your progress and joy in faith, ²⁶so that I may share abundantly in your boasting in Christ Jesus when I come to you again. ²⁷Only, live your life in a manner worthy of the gospel of Christ, so that, whether I come and see you or am absent and hear about you, I will know that you are standing firm in one spirit, striving side by side with one mind for the faith of the gospel, ²⁸and are in no way intimidated by your opponents. For them this is evidence of their destruction, but of your salvation. And this is God's doing. ²⁹For he has graciously granted you the privilege not only of believing in Christ, but of suffering for him as well—³⁰since you are having the same struggle that you saw I had and now hear that I still have. (Philippians 1:21-30 from *New Revised Standard Version*)

In my sermon for those churches that day, I talked about the little church in Philippi—how they had loved and depended upon Paul for his teaching and leadership, but now Paul was in jail. I compared that to their longtime pastor leaving them with all the good memories. I said,

In the Philippi church, everywhere they looked they saw reminders of Paul. Any conflict that arose—what would Paul do? But Paul was gone. Paul was in jail.

It is the same with you. Everywhere you look you see signs of your beloved pastor's presence. But he is gone. He's not in jail, but he is gone. And then a young man agreed to come. You met him, liked him, but he decided not to come. He's gone.

You might have asked yourself last night as you went to bed, "What can possibly happen that can be any worse?" And today you come to church and find an old White preacher in your pulpit."

The congregation erupted in laughter. To say the ice was broken would be an understatement. I continued the sermon, ending with,

You have Christ!

Paul's in prison, but . . .
You have Christ!

Your pastor left for a bigger church but . . .
You have Christ!

The young pastor did not come, but . . .
You have Christ!

3. An Unexpected Opportunity

Why in the world am I getting a letter from the bishop? I questioned. *What have I done now? Something about my pension, maybe?*

Upon reading the letter, I learned that I had been approved (all expenses paid) for a training seminar for preparing pastors to be Interim Ministry Specialists.

Something I didn't even know existed.

Maybe God has other things I need to do, I thought. *Sounded promising.*

I signed up.

Phase I of the program was a four-day introduction. Phase II required a six-months time of working and experiencing the program in the participant's appointment.

Problem was, I had retired and didn't have an appointment—not until my district superintendent asked me to fill in at a White church. The church and pastor had been having problems and the pastor had taken a month's leave of absence to rest and think about solutions.

The superintendent instructed me to do nothing but go to the church each Sunday morning, preach during the 11:00 o'clock service, and go home.

No hospital visits. No counseling. No meetings.

The church had a pastor. I was to fill the pulpit only.

As I was writing my sermon during the first week, I remembered the time when the White elder had asked me that asinine question during my annual meeting with the District Committee on Ordained

Ministry: "Do you think you could preach at a White church?" (Gleaning #34).

Now here I was at Providence United Methodist Church in Statesville after seven years at the African American churches and a few months of preaching at two other African American churches. For a month I had gotten along well with the people at Providence, so the district superintendent appointed me as interim pastor from November 2004 through June 2005. This gave me a place to complete the Interim Ministry Specialist program.

Well, I did it!

I successfully preached in a White church, enjoying God's leading and teaching and watching people work together, visiting hospital patients and shut-ins, and implementing many of the ideas and suggestions that I had gleaned from training in the Interim Ministry Specialist program.

I was a pastor in a White church.

Imagine that!

In the spring of 2005, I committed an unpardonable sin for an interim pastor: I continued after my contracted time was up.

A letter-writing campaign from church members to the district superintendent had urged him to consider me for a full-time appointment in July. Although he had to go to considerable effort to jump through all the hoops to get me out of retirement and reinstated as a full-time local pastor, he made it happen.

I stayed at Providence for almost nine years until, as per UMC's rules, I was obliged to retire at 72.

Reflections by the Lake

On the first day of my second retirement from the United Methodist Church, I sat on our screened-in porch watching raindrops make ripples as they fell upon the lake—little circles that went on and on until they hit some obstacle and were dispersed.

I reflected over my years as a seminary student and through my life and career as a pastor, counselor, and friend to members of my congregations and other people I met along my journey.

Three years at Hood and seven years in the Black churches changed my outlook on life. I guess it would be more truthful to say they changed my life.

I didn't go to seminary to become a pastor of African American churches. It was not what I set out to do. I went for an education. Being the only White student and being in my fifties, I might have had a different outlook on life than other students. I desired to grow in spirit and knowledge of things pertaining to my faith.

In hindsight, I'm not all that sure of what a seminary education can do or does do to one's faith.

Did I really want my eyes to be opened to the *others* of the world, as they were opened? Did I want my faith challenged as it was? Had I expected to become so uncomfortable in my complacency?

I entered seminary determined to stay separate, aloof—to sit in the back of classrooms, study, do my work, and graduate the same person as I entered, only smarter.

I failed.

Looking back at what I had never expected, I now realize that since I made the decision to follow where I was led, how could I be surprised at where I ended up?

A person cannot associate with others without being changed. By my senior year at Hood, Blacks and White (me) could all talk openly to one another without fear of hurting feelings or stepping on toes. We exchanged ideas, philosophies, and explained customs.

As I have changed over the years, so has Hood. In 1998, the year after I graduated, the seminary was accredited by the Association of Theological Schools in the United States and Canada. In 1999, it was approved by the University Senate of the United Methodist Church to prepare ministers for ordination in that body. Since 2002, Hood has offered a Doctor of Ministry degree. In 2005, it moved to a completely new state-of-the-art campus.

(See http://www.hood.edu/History.cfm.)

While visiting the campus recently, I felt envious of the camaraderie among present-day students. I miss the in-depth discussions and the opportunity to hear ideas and comments from a wide base of intellects.

More Caucasians attend now; more women.

Enrollment has increased approximately ten-fold since I graduated with only 12 members in my class.

In my opinion, Hood Theological Seminary is one of the best schools of its kind and I credit the improvement since I was there to one person who came to the seminary the same year I did as the Academic Dean and later became President: Dr. Albert J. D. Aymer.

This man of God had sacrificed much to come to Hood. His enthusiasm and hard work propelled Hood into a school with a great future to compliment its storied past.

It has been my honor and privilege to know him and to call him "Friend."

I assume that my seven years in a cross-racial ministry were somewhat different from what they would have been in a predominantly White church. But I'm not sure if the differences would have out-weighed the similarities.

They were years of learning—learning about who I was as much as who my congregations were.

They were years of learning to accept differences, to accept challenges.

They were years filled with some disappointment and sadness.

But mostly they were years of revelation and change.

I got to know a lot of good people; came to trust and accept a lot of people. And they learned to trust and accept me.

I remember the time I invited members of one of the church councils to come to our house for a dinner meeting. As we were socializing before the meal, I heard one of the guests telling another that she had never been in a White family's house.

This person was the kind of lady who would take anybody, young or old, into her home if they needed a place to go. I remember telling her once: "If Wanda ever kicks me out, I'm gonna come stay with you."

And she said, "That'd be just fine."

A short time before I left the churches, this lady had said to me: "I have a confession to make before you leave. Gotta admit, Rev Ron, when I heard you were coming, I wanted to know: 'Why're they sending a White preacher to us?'"

A racist comment at the time? Perhaps. Perhaps not. But the thing that stands out in my mind is that by the time I concluded my ministry at her church, she felt comfortable enough to talk frankly with me about her initial reaction to getting a White man as a preacher.

A woman who had never been in a White man's home before had taken me into her church home.

I learned that Blacks and Whites are a lot more alike than they are different. And the differences I observed were small—things that shouldn't matter. But in the real world they often do.

Some things Wanda and I thought were differences in culture turned out to be the same. For example, at the first covered-dish dinner we went to at Scotts Chapel, Wanda, expecting to get to dine on "soul" food, looked over the table holding country ham biscuits, turnip greens, fried chicken, deviled eggs, creamed potatoes and gravy, homemade bread, corn and green beans, lima beans, pound cakes, damson pies, persimmon pudding, etc., and said "If that's soul food, then I've been eating it all my life. And it's cooked just like my mama used to cook it."

When you begin to truly understand the stranger, he or she is no longer a stranger. When we can celebrate our differences and laugh at the stereotypical comments we make about them, there is no stranger.

Yes, there are differences and no one should try to change all the differences in the world. Learn from them. Understand the *whys* of them and celebrate our own differences.

When I left the African American churches for my nine years of service with a White church, separations were difficult. Would the friendships I made at Scotts Chapel, Philadelphia, and the Black communities cease?

They couldn't all be maintained, I knew, and a lot of them should not have been maintained because of possible interference in their next pastor's service.

Would all those years be forgotten?

They were not.

Since moving away, I have been asked to participate in funerals, social events, meals, and birthday celebrations for my African American brothers and sisters. I was thrilled this year to receive an invitation to the high school graduation of the young lad who, after the 9-11 service, tugged on my robe and asked, "Rev Ron, am I going to die?" (Gleaning #20).

I was especially honored to be one of several speakers at a Martin Luther King, Jr. community church service about five years after I left.

Even today, it's heartwarming to be greeted by someone I met while I was at Scotts Chapel and Philadelphia who gives me a hug or handshake and recalls an event in his or her life of which I was a part.

So many familiar faces with so many memories.

Not too long ago I was asked to say a few words at the funeral of one of my former members. As I looked at the section where the family sat, I saw this woman's children, grandchildren, great grandchildren and great-great grandchildren. Including the deceased, five generations in this one family had impacted my life as I carried out the activities of Christian life: baptisms, confirmations, marriages, and now the matriarch's funeral.

Once, after I had just preached a sermon that seemed to touch her, she said as I greeted her at the door after the service, "My, my, Rev Ron. You're getting blacker every year."

I took that as a compliment.

I remember Pastor Paul's altar call at my home church (See First Call – Adolescence.) To have one was unheard of at that time and in that place. Then years later, as a pastor myself, I had altar calls every Sunday.

I also remember Pastor Doris Weddington's method of preparing for funeral services. She believed in comparing personal information gleaned from the deceased families' memories to the similarities of life and death for us all, as I do now.

Paul and Doris have both died, but that's the way of life, isn't it?

A way we shall all travel.

No difference in racial equality in death, is there?

Do things change?

Of course. All things change, but it's like the periwinkle on the edge of my yard that I encourage to fill in the natural area. It grows so slowly. It takes time and it can't be forced.

Look at some of the purely political programs designed to bring people together. You can try to force them together, but that doesn't necessarily bring them together.

It's like the United Methodist Church appointing me pastor of two African American churches. No one told them why I was sent to them. No one discussed it with them other than to imply, "You're small, few financial resources, no one else available. Here he is."

The United Methodist Church does a fantastic job of inclusion. But some things may never change. In my case, I truly loved my congregations and they loved me, but in worship style there is a difference and if I had tried to preach in the style my church members were accustomed to, I would have been a phony and their faith and trust in me would probably have been shattered.

We are who we are.

We are different and that should be acceptable.

Life is too short to quibble about a person's skin color or style of preaching.

I know that I'm a better person for having had the opportunity to work in a cross-racial ministry, and I trust that Scotts Chapel and Philadelphia are better off for our experiences together.

When I began to write this book, I thought it would be about my experiences as a White in a Black world—at Hood as its only White Student and then as the White pastor at two African American churches.

Good story for sure. Don't know how many people, Black and White, have suggested I write a book about my experiences in seminary and ministry.

Well, as those of you who have written books know, what you meant to say is not always the way it comes out. And also the way you say anything can be subject to misinterpretation.

After having read my manuscript up to this point, I was thinking ...

It's all going to go back to racism—racism in my specific life's journey, racism in seminaries and organized churches, and racism in society in general.

I've tried to write about events as I perceived them. Although my understanding of racism directed by Whites toward Blacks comes through loud and clear, I also wrote about racism from another perspective—with me as a White man as the target.

Dictionary.com gives three definitions of racism:

1. a belief or doctrine that inherent differences among the various human races determine cultural or individual achievement, usually involving the idea that one's own <u>race</u> is superior and has the right to rule others.
2. a policy, system of government, etc., based upon or fostering such a doctrine; discrimination.
3. hatred or intolerance of another race or other races.

Consistent with definitions one and two, several online articles suggest that to be racist one has to hold power, often implying that only Whites can be racist because they hold power.

In my experience that's not true.

I held no power over anyone when the Black upperclass students at Hood ignored me (Wondering in a Strange Land #1).

I held no power when the elders of the Black church where I opened their revival made it plain to me that I should not be there (Gleaning #7).

I held no power when the Black pastor made it clear I was not welcomed at the funeral (Gleaning #18).

I held no power when I was "a White man" in Mr. and Mrs. Rucker's home (Gleaning #26).

I can understand that perhaps I was resented because of what those people perceived me to represent.

Still, to me, no matter how you try to whitewash the fence, it's still dirty underneath.

Racism is racism and I believe all people are capable of racism. Power can be taken or seen in any situation, so racism is not a respecter of race.

The Black upperclass students at Hood had power because they led the school.

The African American pastor at the funeral had power because of his office.

The elders of the Black church had power because they ran the church.

Everyone has power over somebody, somewhere, sometime.

The third definition more aptly describes my experiences as a target of racism in seminary and outside my own churches in my cross-racial ministry. I never felt like a victim of racism at Scotts Chapel and Philadelphia.

Time is precious. We waste so much of it in fruitless endeavors. One of the biggest wastes of time, energy, and resources is racism. If we could ever truly love our neighbors there is no end to what we could accomplish. But we don't do that. Instead we separate ourselves, put down what we don't understand and, worst of all, refuse to open our hearts and minds to the stranger at our door.

As the rain stopped and the ripples on the lake smoothed out, I continued to reminisce about my cross-racial ministry, remembering three gleanings I had not mentioned in my memoir.

First

At a meeting where a group of White pastors were discussing how to bring the races closer together, a woman said, "I've invited some of the African American people I know to my church up town, but they won't come. How can we ever get together?"

I wonder if she even realized her statement had racial tones to it. I wonder if she ever entertained the possibility of joining her Black friends at their churches.

Is that a barrier that can be overcome in dealing with cross-racial ministries? It's possible but, in my opinion, it would have to be because of a heart-to-heart commitment between both races, not an edict handed down by leaders of an organized church body to combat the sin of racism.

Second

In addition to participating at the revivals mentioned in Gleanings #7 and #33, my church choirs and I were often invited to participate in revival services held by other Black churches in the community. One such occasion I vividly remember.

My role was to read the scripture and offer a prayer. I arrived early and one of the ushers led me to the pastor's study. The pastor, in his early eighties I would guess, gave me a strong hug of welcome and introduced me to the evangelist for the week, a man who was in his early nineties and the pastor of two small churches.

The three of us talked a little about the service, before the conversation turned to the scriptures and their meanings and relationship to today's world.

I sat and listened. I was a youngster compared to these men—young in age, young in experience, young in understanding of the scriptures. And, as I did as a youngster, I kept my mouth shut and listened and learned.

The following week I met with one of my White clergy friends in his study. I had always cherished our stimulating conversations about theology, books we've read, common problems as pastors, and current events in the community and the world.

I told him about my experience with the two elderly Black ministers and he responded:

"Ron, I feel like such a phony when talking about people like that. These aged men believe so strongly and have endured so much. Their faith is so real to them. When we finally make it to heaven, these are the men who will already be there preparing the way for us. Their light will lighten the path for us all."

Looking out the window over the church's cemetery, he paused. Then this highly intelligent man, a gifted speaker with a Ph.D. in Religion, said, "Ron, I could not do what you're doing."

Why would he say that? I wondered. *What was I doing that he could not do? Why would such a gifted individual feel incompetent to do what I do?*

Do what? Be a pastor of Black churches?

What was it he felt he could not do and why would he feel that way?

Third

"You ain't *my* preacher," Miss Maggie had said when I originally visited her in the nursing home (Gleaning #6).

On my second visit I had walked down the hallway, communion kit under my arm and good intentions in my heart. I tapped on her door and entered the room. She was sitting in her chair staring into space. I sat with her for a while, saying nothing. Then facing her, I asked, "Miss Maggie, do you know who I am?"

She squinted her eyes, looked intently at me and with her toothless smile answered slowly but clearly:

"Yes Rev . . . you're *my* preacher."

A Testimonial

This book boldly illustrates the perspectives of the Rev. Ron Karriker—the man, the husband, and the pastor.

His impressions of the African American church are realistic and empathetic, and collectively, his personal, educational, and professional experiences undoubtedly contributed to his effectiveness as a pastor.

Mrs. Edith Martin Derr
M. A., Columbia University Teachers College
Member of Scotts Chapel United Methodist Church since 1947

Appendix: The Terminology Dilemma

Some people prefer "Black"; others prefer "African American" when describing Americans of African descent. When I began compiling the gleanings for this book, I phoned a friend in academia and asked: "Which term do you think is most appropriate when writing about my cross-racial ministry?"

He answered, "My first thoughts—we're all children of God. It shouldn't matter." After a brief pause he added, "The most acceptable term is African American."

(After completing the manuscript for *You Ain't My Preacher*, I learned that "there is a recent trend toward omitting the hyphen, possibly in reaction to the belittling phrase 'hyphenated Americans.'"[3] Thus, I have chosen to omit the hyphen in this book).

I assumed my friend was thinking this book would be purely academic. Not so. I have written it for a general audience and in my own way of talking, frequently using incomplete sentences.

---

3   See http://public.wsu.edu/~brians/errors/african.html

"A lot of my church members didn't like to be called African Americans," I responded to my friend. "They said they preferred to be called Americans."

"Older people?" he asked.

"Yes, they were." I failed to tell him that some of the members of the Black churches I served still used the terms "Colored" and "Negro" when talking about members of their own race.

We caught up on mutual interests, and I thanked him for his help with my dilemma.

Sometime later I called on my friend, Google.

The search engine showed me a scholarly article[4] in which the author chronicles when and why racial labels were changed.

"Colored" and "Negro" were used before the civil rights movement when they were replaced with "Black" as the preferred label. This term went unchallenged until 1988 when Jesse Jackson, as spokesperson of the National Urban Coalition, proposed that "African American" (a term that was used in the late 1700s) replace it.[5]

---

4   Tom W. Smith, "Changing Racial Labels: From 'Colored' to 'Negro' to 'Black' to 'African American,'" *Public Opinion Quarterly* 56 (1992): 496-514; found at http://publicdata.norc.org:41000/gss/DOCUMENTS/REPORTS/Topical_Repo rts/TR22.pdf (accessed 4/15/2013.

5   Ibid., pp. 499-503.

By 1992, "African American" had been accepted by the mass media as the preferred term. Some periodicals used it exclusively as a racial label for the group that had previously been called "Colored" or "Negro" or "Black."[6]

My African American church members (1997-2004) used the terms interchangeably. Consistent with the findings of a 2007 Gallup Poll,[7] they didn't seem to care which term was used. In this poll, a random sample of Black Americans were asked:

> Some people say the term 'African-American' should be used instead of the word 'black.' Which term do you prefer—'African-American' or 'black' or does it not matter to you either way?

Twenty-seven percent of respondents preferred "African-American"; 13% preferred "Black"; 61% said it didn't matter. The pollsters concluded:

> The results of available survey research indicate no strong consensus among the American Black

---

6   Ibid. See entire article for a detailed discussion of the pros and cons of replacing "Black" with "African American."

7   Frank Newport, *Black or African American?*: Gallup News Service, September 28, 2007, http://www.gallup.com/poll/28816/black-african-american.aspx (accessed 4/15/13).

community for how their racial group should be described.[8]

I have long been aware that the label "Black" is offensive to some people; "African American," to others.

I am also aware that since the 1980s, the term African American is often considered politically correct. But this might be changing. In a 2012 Associated Press article, the author writes:

> The labels used to describe Americans of African descent mark the movement of a people from the slave house to the White House. Today, many are resisting this progression by holding on to a name from the past: 'black.'[9]

Since there appears to be no consensus in the American Black community or in the media regarding the use of "Black" or "African American," I decided to use the terms interchangeably in this book. I capitalized "Black" and "White" and "Colored" in my original writing when the terms refer to people.

---

8   Ibid.

9   Jesse Washington, *Some Blacks Insist: "I'm Not African American"*: Associated Press –*February 4, 2012*, http://news.yahoo.com/blacks-insist-im-not-african-american-181257715.html (accessed 4/12/13).

In some of my early anecdotes, using "Black" or "African American" would not have been congruent with the time an event took place; therefore, I used the terms "Colored" and "Negro" to apply to Americans of African descent in the years before the term "Black" became preferable.

Understanding the derogatory nature of what has come to be called the "N-word" and how repulsive the word is to me, I didn't spell it out but instead used [N-word] to illustrate some of my cultural heritage regarding race.

CPSIA information can be obtained at www.ICGtesting.com
Printed in the USA
LVOW08s0030210813

348779LV00001B/1/P